The
SmartCook
Collection

Fish

The SmartCook Collection
Fish

LONDON, NEW YORK, MUNICH,
MELBOURNE, and DELHI

Senior Editor   Anja Schmidt
Art Director   Dirk Kaufman
Designer   Bill Miller
Design Assistant   Adrian Peters
DTP Coordinator   Kathy Farias
Production Manager   Ivor Parker
Executive Managing Editor   Sharon Lucas
Publisher   Carl Raymond

U.S. Recipe Adapter   Rick Rodgers

First published in 2004 by BBC Books
BBC Worldwide Limited
Woodlands, 80 Wood Lane
London W12 0TT

Published in the United States in 2006 by
DK Publishing
375 Hudson Street,
New York, New York 10014

Printed and bound in China by Toppan Printing Co.,
(Shenzen) Ltd.
Color separation by Radstock Reproduction Ltd
Midsomer Norton
Additional color work by Colourscan, Singapore

Cover and title-page photographs: Michael Paul
For further photographic credits, see page 136

Some recipes in this book contain raw eggs,
which are know to contain the potentially harmful
salmonella bacterium. Do not serve dishes made
with raw eggs to the very young, elderly, or those
with compromised immune systems.

Discover more at
www.dk.com

Introduction

When I look back over my years of cookbook writing, I have to admit that very often, decisions about what to do have sprung from what my own particular needs are. As a very busy person who has to work, run a home, and cook, I felt it was extremely useful to have, for instance, summer recipes in one book – likewise winter and Christmas, giving easy access to those specific seasons.

The SmartCook Collection has come about for similar reasons. Thirty-three years of recipe writing have produced literally thousands of recipes. So I now feel what would be really helpful is to create a kind of ordered library (so I don't have to rack my brains and wonder which book this or that recipe is in!). Thus, if I want to make a fish recipe, I don't have to look through the fish sections of various books, but have all of them in one convenient collection.

In compiling these collections, I have chosen what I think are the best and most popular recipes and, at the same time, have added some that are completely new. It is my hope that those who have not previously tried my recipes will now have smaller collections to sample, and that those dedicated followers will appreciate an ordered library to provide easy access and a reminder of what has gone before and may have been forgotten.

Delia Smith

Conversion Tables

All these are approximate conversions, which have either been rounded up or down. In a few recipes it has been necessary to modify them very slightly. Never mix metric and imperial measures in one recipe; stick to one system or the other.

All spoon measurements used throughout this book are level unless specified otherwise.

All butter is salted unless specified otherwise.

All recipes have been double-tested, using a standard convection oven.

Weights

½ oz	10 g
¾	20
1	25
1½	40
2	50
2½	60
3	75
4	110
4½	125
5	150
6	175
7	200
8	225
9	250
10	275
12	350
1 lb	450
1 lb 8 oz	700
2	900
3	1.35 kg

Volume

2 fl oz	55 ml
3	75
5 (¼ pint)	150
10 (½ pint)	275
1 pint	570
1¼	725
1¾	1 litre
2	1.2
2½	1.5
4	2.25

Dimensions

⅛ inch	3 mm
¼	5
½	1 cm
¾	2
1	2.5
1¼	3
1½	4
1¾	4.5
2	5
2½	6
3	7.5
3½	9
4	10
5	13
5¼	13.5
6	15
6½	16
7	18
7½	19
8	20
9	23
9½	24
10	25.5
11	28
12	30

Oven temperatures

Gas mark 1	275°F	140°C
2	300	150
3	325	170
4	350	180
5	375	190
6	400	200
7	425	220
8	450	230
9	475	240

Contents

White-fleshed Fish page 7
Salmon and Trout page 41
Oily and Other Seafood page 71
Smoked Fish page 99

Fish Extras page 125
Index page 132

White-fleshed Fish

Fried Flounder Fillets
with an Herbed Polenta Crust
Serves 2

2 skinless flounder fillets
(about 6 oz each)

½ cup polenta (yellow cornmeal)

1 teaspoon finely chopped fresh
rosemary or 2 teaspoons finely
snipped chives

1 teaspoon finely chopped fresh
thyme

2 garlic cloves, very finely chopped

Grated zest and juice of 2 small
lemons

Salt and freshly ground black
pepper to taste

1 large egg

2 tablespoons olive oil

A good way to avoid making breadcrumbs, and therefore save time, is to keep a package of polenta (Italian yellow cornmeal, although stone-ground domestic cornmeal will do) in the pantry. It makes an excellent coating for all types of fish; here it's mixed with garlic, herbs, and lemon to coat flounder fillets. You can use lemon sole instead of flounder if you prefer.

1. This couldn't be simpler. Start by wiping the flounder fillets with paper towels. Combine the polenta, rosemary, thyme, and garlic on a flat plate. Then add the lemon zest and season with salt and pepper and mix it all evenly. Beat the egg in a shallow dish, dip the fillets in the egg, and coat them with the polenta mixture, pressing it on well.

2. Now take a very large skillet and heat the oil in it over high heat. When it is good and hot, add the fish, then turn the heat down to medium. Cook the fish for 2 or 3 minutes on each side, depending on the thickness. Using a slotted spatula, transfer the fish to paper towels to drain. Serve on hot plates with the lemon juice squeezed over.

Fillets of Sole Véronique
Serves 2

12 cup green grapes, preferably Muscat

2 skinless sole, lemon sole, or flounder fillets (about 4 oz each)

Salt and freshly ground black pepper to taste

1 tablespoon butter, plus a little extra for greasing

1¼ teaspoons chopped fresh tarragon

¾ cup dry vermouth or dry white wine

1 tablespoon plain flour

⅔ cup heavy cream

This famous French classic is extra delicious served with the grapes well chilled, which beautifully complements the warm, rich sauce. However, if you prefer, you could add the grapes to the fish before it goes under the grill.

1.   First, peel the grapes well in advance by placing them in a bowl and pouring boiling water over them. Leave them for 45 seconds, then drain off the water and you will find the skins will slip off easily. Cut the grapes in half, remove the seeds, then return them to the bowl, and cover and chill in the refrigerator until needed.

2.   When you are ready to start cooking the fish, begin by warming a flame-proof serving dish and have a sheet of aluminum foil ready. Then wipe each sole fillet with paper towels. Divide each fillet in half lengthways by cutting along the natural line, so you have 8 fillets. Season them with salt and pepper and roll up tightly, keeping the skinned side on the inside and starting the roll at the narrow end. Next, put a faint smear of butter on the bottom of a medium skillet and arrange the rolled fillets in it. Then sprinkle in the tarragon, followed by the vermouth. Now place the skillet on medium heat and bring it to simmering point. Cover, then put a timer on and poach the fillets for 3 to 4 minutes, depending on their thickness. They should only be half-cooked at this point. While the fish is poaching, preheat the broiler to its highest setting.

3.   Meanwhile, melt the butter in a small saucepan over low heat. Stir in the flour to make a smooth paste and let cook gently, stirring all the time, until it has become a pale straw color. When the fish is cooked, transfer the fillets with a slotted spatula to the warmed serving dish and cover with aluminum foil to keep warm. Reserve the poaching liquid in the skillet and boil it over high heat until reduced to about a third of its original volume. Stir in the cream and bring to a gentle simmer. Gradually whisk the liquid into the flour and butter paste, and cook until you have a thin, creamy sauce. Taste and season with salt and pepper. Pour the sauce over the fish and place it under the preheated broiler, about 4 inches from the source of the heat, and broil for 3 to 4 minutes, until it is glazed golden brown on top. Serve on warmed serving plates.

Pan-Fried Skate Wings with Warm Salsa Verde
Serves 2

For the green salsa

1 medium garlic clove

½ teaspoon salt, preferably
sea salt

¼ cup fresh lime juice
(2 large limes)

2 tablespoons chopped fresh
flat-leaf parsley

2 tablespoons fruity olive oil

4 anchovy fillets, drained and
finely chopped

4 teaspoons bottled capers,
rinsed and drained

1 tablespoon chopped fresh basil

1¼ teaspoons wholegrain mustard

Freshly ground black pepper

For the fish

1 lb skate wings (2 small or
1 large cut in half)

1½ tablespoons all-purpose flour
seasoned with salt and pepper

2 tablespoons peanut or other
flavorless oil

Skate wings have everything going for them. They possess a fine-flavored creamy flesh that comes away from the bone with no fuss, and they're extremely easy to cook. They are excellent pan-fried to a crisp, golden color, with a sharp and quite gutsy sauce poured in at the last moment. Your fish store may only sell filleted skate wings, which will also work with this recipe. Simply cook them for a bit less than the wings on the bone. Serve with a green salad and some boiled tiny new potatoes.

1. I think it's preferable to make the salsa not too far ahead as the parsley tends to discolor, though you could make up most of the salsa in advance and add the parsley at the last moment – either way, it's very quick and easy. All you do is crush the clove of garlic with the salt, using a pestle and mortar (or on a board using the back of a tablespoon) until you get a paste-like consistency. Then simply combine this with all the other salsa ingredients and mix everything very thoroughly.

2. To cook the skate wings, take a very large skillet and put it over low heat to warm up while you wipe the skate wings with paper towels and coat them with a light dusting of the seasoned flour. Now turn the heat up to high, add the oil to the pan and, as soon as it's really hot, add the skate wings. Reduce the heat to medium and cook them for 4 to 5 minutes on each side, depending on their size and thickness. To test if they are cooked, slide the tip of a sharp knife in and push to see if the flesh parts from the bone easily and looks creamy white. Then pour in the salsa around the fish to heat very briefly. It doesn't need to cook but simply to warm a little. Serve the fish immediately with the salsa spooned on top.

Thai Fish Curry with Mango
Serves 4

Two 14-ounce cans unsweetened coconut milk

For the curry paste

1 small onion, peeled and quartered

2 medium red chilies, halved lengthwise and seeds removed

2 lemongrass stalks, tender parts peeled and coarsely chopped

1 inch piece of fresh ginger, peeled and sliced

Grated zest and juice of 1 lime

4 garlic cloves, peeled

3 tablespoons Thai fish sauce

1 teaspoon Asian shrimp paste

For the fish

2 lb firm fish fillets (such as halibut, cod or haddock), skinned and chopped into 1½-inch chunks

1 large ripe mango, peeled and cut into ¾-inch pieces

3 tablespoons chopped fresh cilantro leaves, for serving

You won't believe how utterly simple this recipe is, and yet it tastes exotic and wonderful and, what's more, it can all be prepared well in advance and the fish added about 10 minutes before you want to eat it. Some Thai jasmine rice makes the perfect side dish.

1. Begin by emptying the coconut milk into a large, deep skillet or wok and stir while you bring it to a boil. Reduce the heat to medium and cook until the fat separates from the solids. What will happen is the coconut milk will start to separate, the oil will begin to seep out, and it will reduce. Ignore the curdled look – this is normal. You may also like to note that, when it begins to separate, you can actually hear it give off a crackling noise. This will take 20 minutes or so, and you will have about 2 cups left.

2. Now to make the curry paste, all you do is put everything in a food processor or blender and process until you have a rather coarse, rough-looking paste and everything is perfectly blended.

3. Then, over medium heat, add the curry paste and fish to the coconut milk, and, once it comes to a simmer, cook for 4 minutes. Finally, add the mango and cook for another 2 minutes. Serve the curry with the cilantro sprinkled on top and Thai jasmine rice as an accompaniment.

Note: You can prepare most of the curry in advance. Make everything up, keeping the curry paste covered and refrigerated. Then, 10 minutes before you want to serve, bring the coconut milk back up to the boil and add the curry paste, fish, and mango, as above.

Roasted Monkfish with Romesco Sauce
Serves 6

For the sauce

3 ripe fresh plum tomatoes

3 large garlic cloves, peeled

About 15 whole hazelnuts

2 small dried chilies

1 large egg yolk

1 cup extra virgin olive oil

2 tablespoons sherry vinegar

For the fish

2 lb boned and skinned
monkfish tail

¼ cup extra virgin olive oil

A squeeze of fresh lemon juice

Salt and freshly ground black
pepper to taste

A few sprigs of flat-leaf parsley,
for garnish

Lemon wedges, for serving

Monkfish is a meaty fish that can take a pungent sauce like Romesco. The classic Spanish recipe uses almonds, but this version, supplied by private chef Clare Hunter, substitutes hazelnuts. Serve the monkfish with tiny French Puy lentils cooked in red wine with thyme and dressed with olive oil and balsamic vinegar.

1. First, preheat the oven to 350°F. To make the sauce, put the tomatoes, whole garlic cloves, and hazelnuts into a shallow roasting tray in the oven for 10 minutes, then add the chilies. Cook for another 5 minutes until the hazelnuts are golden brown under their peeling skins. Place the hazelnuts in a clean kitchen towel and rub them against each other to remove as much of the skin as possible. Peel the tomatoes and place them into a blender with the egg yolk, garlic, hazelnuts, and chilies. Blend on high speed and add the olive oil slowly to make a smooth sauce. Next, stir in the vinegar, season lightly with salt and pepper, cover, and set aside.

2. Remove the fish from the refrigerator 30 minutes before you need it, to allow it to lose its chill. When you are ready to cook the fish, increase the oven temperature to 400°F. Lightly brush the fish fillets with some of the olive oil. Heat a large skillet, add the remaining oil and, when it is very hot, add the oiled fillets and lightly brown them on all sides. Transfer them to a rimmed baking sheet and roast in the top third of the oven for 10 to 15 minutes, depending on the thickness of the monkfish. Remove from the oven, season with salt and freshly ground black pepper, and sprinkle with lemon juice. If necessary, reduce the juices from the fish by heating the baking sheet over high heat.

3. Slice the fillets on the diagonal. Place on warmed serving plates and pour a little of the fish juice on top. Serve with the romesco sauce, sprigs of parsley, and lemon wedges.

Seafood Pie with Crisp Potato Topping
Serves 4 to 6

For the rösti caper topping

2 lb baking potatoes, such as russet or Burbank, evenly sized if possible

1 tablespoon bottled capers, rinsed and drained

4 tablespoons butter, melted

For the fish mixture

1¼ cups fish stock or 1 cup bottled clam juice and ¼ cup water

⅔ cup dry white wine

1 bay leaf

Salt and freshly ground black pepper to taste

1 lb 8 oz halibut

6 sea scallops, including the coral, cut in half

6 oz peeled and deveined large shrimp

4 tablespoons butter

¼ cup all-purpose flour

2 tablespoons crème fraîche or heavy cream

6 cornichons, drained, rinsed, and chopped

4 teaspoons chopped fresh parsley

2 teaspoons chopped fresh dill

½ cup (2 oz) shredded sharp Cheddar cheese

This is a perfect recipe for entertaining that needs nothing more to accompany it than a simple green salad. The fish and shellfish can be varied according to what's best in the market, as long as the total weighs 2¼ pounds. Cod or other white, firm-fleshed fish can easily stand in for halibut, and if you can find scallops with the roe attached, use them for an added touch of elegance.

1. Prepare the potatoes by scrubbing them with the skins on. If there are any larger ones, cut them in half. Then cover them in a saucepan with boiling, salted water. Return to the boil and cook them for 12 minutes, covered with the lid. Drain and return to the pot. Cover with a clean kitchen towel and let stand for 10 minutes to absorb excess steam. Peel the potatoes and, using the coarse side of a grater, grate them into long shreds into a bowl. Then add the capers and the melted butter. Using two forks, lightly toss everything together so that the potatoes get a good coating of butter.

2. Meanwhile, heat the wine and fish stock in a medium saucepan, add the bay leaf and some seasoning, then cut the halibut in half if it's a large piece, add it to the saucepan, and poach the fish gently for 5 minutes. It should be slightly undercooked.

3. Use a slotted spatula to transfer the fish to a plate, and strain the poaching liquid through a sieve into a bowl. Rinse the pan you cooked the fish in, melt the butter in it, whisk in the flour, and gently cook for 2 minutes. Then add the poaching liquid little by little, whisking all the time. When you have a smooth sauce, turn the heat to its lowest setting and let it cook for 5 minutes. Then, whisk in the crème fraîche, followed by the cornichons, parsley, and dill. Give it all a good seasoning and remove it from the heat. Now remove the skin from the halibut and divide it into chunks, quite large if possible, and combine the fish with the sauce. Add the raw scallops and shrimp to the fish mixture spoon it into a well-buttered 6- to 8-cup shallow casserole. Sprinkle the potato mixture on top, spreading it out as evenly as possible and not pressing it down too firmly. Finally, scatter the Cheddar over the surface.

4. Preheat the oven to 375°F. Bake the pie in the top third of the oven for 35 to 40 minutes, until the sauce is bubbling and the potatoes are golden brown.

Roast Cod with Sun-Dried Tomato Tapenade
Serves 6

For the tapenade

10 oz sun-dried tomatoes in oil, drained, oil reserved

¾ cup brined black olives, 6 whole olives reserved for garnish, and the remainder drained, pitted, and rinsed

16 fresh basil leaves

2 large garlic cloves, peeled

3 tablespoons bottled capers, drained, rinsed, and patted dry

6 anchovy fillets, including their oil

1½ teaspoons green peppercorns in brine, drained and rinsed

Freshly ground black pepper

For the fish

6 cod or haddock fillets (about 6 oz each each), skinned

Salt and freshly ground black pepper to taste

Bright with flavor and easy to put together in no time at all, this is, quite simply, a fantastic recipe. Everyone will think you spent hours in the kitchen. Serve with rice or potatoes and a simple green vegetable.

1. To make the tapenade – which can be made 2 or 3 days in advance – place all the ingredients (reserve 6 basil leaves), using only 2 tablespoons of the tomato oil and reserving the remainder for later, in a food processor and blend them together to a coarse paste. It's important not to overprocess; the ingredients should retain some of their identity.

2. Preheat the oven to 400°F. When you're ready to cook the fish, wipe the fillets with paper towels and season them with salt and pepper. Fold each by tucking the thin end into the center, then the thick end on top of that so you have a neat, slightly rounded shape. Turn them over and place on an oiled rimmed baking sheet. Divide the tapenade mixture equally among them, using it as a topping. Press it on quite firmly with your hands, then lightly roughen the surface with a fork. Dip the 6 reserved basil leaves in a little of the reserved tomato oil and place one on top of each piece of fish, following that with a reserved olive. Now roast in the top third of the oven for 20 for 25 minutes. Serve immediately.

Steamed Fish Rolls
with Ginger, Scallions, and Sesame
Serves 4

One 2½-inch piece of fresh ginger, peeled

3 garlic cloves

2 scallions

4 teaspoons sesame seeds

2 teaspoons Asian dark sesame oil

2 teaspoons peanut or other flavorless oil

Juice of 1 lemon

1 tablespoon Japanese soy sauce

1 lb 8 oz lemon sole or flounder fillets, skinned and cut lengthways down the natural dividing line

A few large lettuce leaves or oiled aluminum foil, for lining the steamer

Salt and freshly ground black pepper to taste

Light and tempting, this can serve as a quick family supper dish or part of a larger Asian meal for entertaining. All you need is a steamer – either Chinese bamboo or all-purpose metal will do. Serve with steamed or fried rice.

1. Begin this by having a little chopping session. First, the ginger, which should be thinly sliced, then cut into very fine shreds. The garlic needs to be finely chopped, as do the scallions, making sure you include the green parts as well.

2. Now place a medium skillet over medium heat and, when it's hot, add the sesame seeds and toast them in the dry pan, shaking it from time to time until they're a golden brown color – this takes only 1 to 2 minutes. Now transfer the seeds to a bowl.

3. Next add the peanut and sesame oils to the pan and, over medium heat, add and gently cook the chopped garlic and ginger – they need to be pale gold but not too brown, so take care not to have the heat too high. After that, add these to the toasted seeds, along with any oil left in the pan, then mix in the lemon juice, soy sauce, and chopped scallions.

4. Now season the fish with salt and pepper. Spread three-quarters of the mixture over the surface of each skinned side, roll them up quite firmly into little rolls, then spoon the rest of the mixture on top of each roll. All this can be prepared in advance, as long as the fish is kept covered in the refrigerator.

5. Then, when you're ready to cook the fish, line the base of the steamer with the lettuce leaves (or the foil, if you don't have any). Place the fish on top, cover with a lid, and steam over boiling water for 8 to 10 minutes, or until the fish looks barely opaque when flaked in the center with the tip of a small sharp knife. Serve at once.

Flaky Fish Galette
Serves 4

For the pastry

12 tablespoons (1½ sticks) butter

1¾ cups all-purpose flour, plus a little extra for dusting

A pinch of salt

For the filling

16 oz any firm white-fleshed fish steaks (such as haddock, cod, or whiting)

about 2 cups milk

2 tablespoons butter, plus more for the baking sheet

2 tablespoons all-purpose flour

2 large eggs, hard-boiled and chopped

4 cornichons, drained and chopped

2 tablespoons chopped fresh parsley

1 tablespoon bottled capers, rinsed, drained, and chopped

1 tablespoon fresh lemon juice

Salt and freshly ground black pepper to taste

1 large egg, beaten, for the glaze

Here's a great way to transform a humble fish like haddock, cod, or whiting into a lovely savory pastry that's really something special.

1. To make the pastry, first of all, wrap the butter in a piece of aluminum foil. Place it in the freezer for 30 to 45 minutes. When you are ready to make the pastry, sift the flour and salt into a large, roomy bowl. Take the butter out of the freezer, fold back the foil and hold it in the foil, which will protect it from your warm hands. Then, using the coarse side of a grater placed in the bowl of flour, grate the butter, dipping the edge of the butter into the flour several times to make it easier to grate. What you will end up with is a large pile of grated butter sitting in the middle of the flour.

2. Now take a metal icing spatula and start to distribute the gratings into the flour – don't use your hands, just keep trying to coat all the pieces of butter with flour. Then sprinkle 2–3 tablespoons of cold water all over, continue to use the palette knife to bring the whole thing together, and finish off, using your hands. If you need a bit more moisture, that's fine – just remember that the dough should come together in such a way that it leaves the bowl fairly clean, with no bits of loose butter or flour anywhere. Now pop it into a self-sealing plastic bag and refrigerate for at least 30 minutes before using.

3. To make the filling, place the fish in a medium saucepan with just enough milk to cover it, bring to boil over medium heat, cover, and simmer gently for about 5 to 10 minutes. Now strain off the milk into a glass liquid measuring cup. When the fish is cool enough to handle, flake it into large pieces (discarding all the bones and skin), place it in a bowl and set aside. Next, melt the butter in the same saucepan and stir in the flour. Cook for about 2 minutes over medium heat. Gradually add 1¼ cups of the milk the fish was cooked in, stirring all the time. Bring the sauce to the boil, then simmer gently for 6 minutes, stirring from time to time. Take the pan off the heat and add the flaked fish, eggs, cornichons, parsley, and capers, then add the lemon juice, and season with salt and pepper to taste. Cover and let stand at room temperature until the mixture has cooled completely.

4. When you're ready to cook the pie, preheat the oven to 425°F. Grease a large rimmed baking sheet well. On a lightly floured surface, roll out the pastry to a 12-inch square, trimming, if necessary. Transfer the square to the greased baking sheet, then place the fish mixture in the center. Glaze around the edge of the pastry with the beaten egg, then pull the opposite corners of the pastry to the center and pinch all the edges together firmly, so you have a square with pinched edges in the shape of a cross. Glaze all over with some beaten egg, decorate with any pastry trimmings, and glaze these, too. Bake the pie for 30 minutes or until the pastry is well risen and golden.

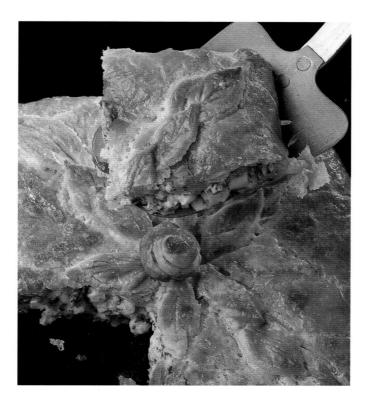

Baked Fish Fillets with a Parmesan Crust
Serves 4

4 tablespoons butter, melted, plus a little extra for brushing and drizzling

8 sole, lemon sole, or flounder fillets (about 1½ lb)

Salt and freshly ground black pepper as needed

1 cup fresh bread crumbs, made from 3–4 slices slightly stale, firm white bread in a blender or food processor

¾ cup (3 oz) freshly grated Parmesan cheese

2 tablespoon chopped fresh parsley

To garnish

1 lemon, cut into quarters

A few sprigs of fresh parsley

Savory fish with a crisp cheesy crust will win over the whole family. You can use this same coating with a thicker fish, such as cod or haddock; just allow about 5 minutes longer for cooking. This doesn't need a sauce, but a green salad with a lemony dressing would be a good accompaniment.

1. First of all, preheat the oven to 450°F. Line a large rimmed baking sheet with aluminum foil. Brush the foil generously with melted butter. Now wipe the fish with paper towels, then lay it on the foil and season with salt and black pepper to taste.

2. Next, mix the bread crumbs, Parmesan cheese, and parsley in a bowl. Add 3 tablespoons of the melted butter, ½ teaspoon salt and some pepper, and mix again until the crumbs are evenly moistened.

3. Now spread the crumb mixture over the fish fillets and drizzle them with the remaining melted butter. Place the baking sheet in the top third of the oven and bake for 7 to 8 minutes, or until the crumbs have turned golden brown. Serve with the lemon quarters for squeezing over the fish and parsley sprigs as garnish.

Pepper-Crusted Monkfish with Red Pepper Relish
Serves 4

For the red pepper relish

1 tablespoon olive oil

2 medium red peppers, deseeded and cut into strips

2 medium tomatoes, skinned and halved, or canned Italian tomatoes would be fine

1 plump garlic clove, peeled

3 anchovy fillets, drained and chopped

1 tablespoon balsamic vinegar

Salt and freshly ground black pepper to taste

For the fish

2 lb skinned and boned monkfish fillets

5 teaspoons mixed whole peppercorns (a combination of black, white, pink, and green peppercorns, often sold as pepper medley)

3 tablespoons all-purpose flour, seasoned with 1 teaspoon salt

4 tablespoons olive oil

Sprigs of watercress or fresh cilantro leaves, for garnish

Monkfish can be quite expensive, but there is no waste with head or bones. It has a lovely, firm, meaty texture, and this particular recipe is a superb choice for someone who wants to cook something quite special but has very little time. The chunks of fish are coated with crushed peppercorns, and this simplest of sauces not only tastes divine, but looks amazingly colorful in contrast.

1. Begin the relish by heating the oil in a medium saucepan. When it's really hot, add the strips of pepper and toss them around, keeping them on the move so they get nicely toasted and browned at the edges. Then add the tomatoes, then the garlic and the anchovies. Give it all a good stir, put on a lid and, keeping the heat at its lowest possible setting, let the whole thing stew gently, stirring once or twice, for 25 minutes or until the peppers are soft. Then process the mixture to a coarse purée in a blender or food processor. Taste and season with salt and freshly ground pepper, then transfer into a serving bowl and stir in the balsamic vinegar. It is now ready for serving and can be made a few hours in advance, kept at room temperature.

2. To cook the fish, first cut it into rounds about ¾-inch thick. Crush the peppercorns with a pestle and mortar – or using the end of a rolling pin in a small bowl – to a fairly course texture, then combine them with the seasoned flour.

3. Next, heat the oil until very hot in a large skillet pan. Dip each piece of fish in the flour and peppercorn mixture, pressing them gently on all sides to get an even coating. Now cook the fish in two batches, for about 2 to 3 minutes on each side, until they're tinged nicely brown. Cover the first batch loosely with aluminum foil to keep it warm while you cook the second. Serve, garnished with watercress or fresh cilantro sprigs, and the sauce handed around separately.

Thai Fish Cakes with Sesame-Lime Dipping Sauce
Serves 4 as a main course or 8 as a starter

3 tablespoons fresh cilantro leaves, plus sprigs for garnish

½ small red bell pepper, deseeded and roughly chopped

1 stem lemongrass, tender bulb part peeled and roughly chopped

One ½-inch thick slice fresh ginger, peeled and roughly chopped

1 plump garlic clove, peeled

1 medium red chili, deseeded

zest of 1 lime (reserve the juice for the sauce)

2 fresh kaffir lime leaves, roughly chopped, or the grated zest of 1 lime

½ cup coconut milk powder, available at Thai markets (optional)

1 lb any white fish fillets (cod works well), skinned and cut into chunks

Salt and freshly ground black pepper to taste

2 tablespoons all-purpose flour, lightly seasoned with salt and pepper

2 or 3 tablespoons peanut or other flavorless oil, for frying

For the dipping sauce

2 teaspoon sesame seeds

2 tablespoons Asian dark sesame oil

2 tablespoons fresh lime juice

2 tablespoons Japanese soy sauce

4 teaspoons Thai fish sauce

2 medium red chilies, deseeded and very finely chopped

While this ingredient list looks long, these little fish cakes can be formed and cooked very quickly. Besides serving as either a first course or light main dish, they make a terrific hors d'oeuvres to serve with drinks. If you choose to offer them as an appetizer, make them smaller – about 1 inch in diameter.

1. To make the fish cakes you first of all need to put the cilantro, red bell pepper, lemongrass, ginger, garlic, chili, lime zest, and lime leaves (if using) into a food processor, then pulse to blend everything fairly finely. After that, add the chunks of fish, and pulse again briefly until the fish is blended in.

2. Then transfer the mixture to a bowl, add some salt and pepper, and shape the fish cakes into 24 fairly small, thin, flattish, round shapes about 2 inches in diameter. If you like, you can make them ahead to this stage, but spread them out in a single layer, cover with plastic wrap, and refrigerate until needed.

3. Meanwhile, make the dipping sauce. To do this, first of all begin by toasting the sesame seeds. Preheat a small, solid skillet over medium heat, then add the sesame seeds and stir them until they are evenly toasted. As soon as they begin to splutter and pop and turn golden, they're ready – this will take 1 or 2 minutes. Then transfer them to a bowl and simply stir in sesame oil, lime juice, soy sauce, fish sauce, and chili. Divide the sauce between individual small bowls for dipping.

4. When you're ready to cook the fish cakes, first coat them in the seasoned flour, then heat 2 tablespoons of the oil in a large skillet over high heat. When it's really hot, turn the heat down to medium and fry the fish cakes briefly for about 30 seconds on each side until they are pale gold. You will need to cook them in several batches, adding a little more oil, if necessary. As they cook, transfer to a warm plate and keep warm. Serve with the dipping sauce, garnished with the reserved cilantro sprigs.

Fish Fillets with Cheddar-Cilantro Crust
Serves 4

4 skinless fish fillets (such as cod, haddock, or whiting, about 7 oz each)

¼ cup Cilantro and Lime Tartar Sauce (page 129)

¼ cup fresh white or whole-wheat breadcrumbs, made from firm, slightly stale bread in the blender or food processor

⅓ cup finely shredded sharp Cheddar cheese

4 teaspoons chopped fresh cilantro

Grated zest of 1 lime

A pinch of cayenne pepper

2 tablespoons butter, cut into small cubes, plus more for the broiler pan

Salt and freshly ground black pepper to taste

If you have a jar of lovely Cilantro and Lime Tartar Sauce (page 129), a good way to use it is to spread it on to some fish fillets, then sprinkle with cheese and breadcrumbs and pop them under a preheated broiler. You'll have one of the fastest and most delectable suppers imaginable. Serve with buttered new potatoes with chives.

1. Begin by lining a broiler pan with oil and smearing the foil with a trace of butter. Wipe the fish with paper towels to get them as dry as possible, then place them in the broiler pan. Season with salt and pepper, then spread equal amounts of the tartar sauce all over the top of each fillet.

2. Now, in a bowl, mix the breadcrumbs, cheese, cilantro, lime zest, and cayenne together, then sprinkle equal amounts over the fish as evenly as possible. Dot with a little butter.

3. Preheat the broiler on high. Place the broiler pan as far from the heat as possible (about 6–8 inches) and broil the fish for 10 to 15 minutes, depending on its thickness – it should be just cooked through and the top should be crispy and golden. Serve with a plain lettuce salad.

Steamed Cod with Nori and Soba Noodle Salad
Serves 2

10 oz skinless cod fillet

1 tablespoon Japanese soy sauce

1 tablespoon Thai fish sauce

2 sheets toasted nori seaweed

For the noodle salad

7 oz dried soba noodles

3 tablespoons Japanese soy sauce

3 tablespoons fresh lime juice

½ teaspoon Asian dark sesame oil

A pinch of salt

About 6 sprigs of fresh watercress, for garnish

2 tablespoons Japanese pickled ginger, for serving

This is a wonderful combination of flavors and textures – and only contains half a teaspoon of oil between two people. The photograph shows green-tea soba noodles (buckwheat noodles made with green tea) but if you find these difficult to get, ordinary soba noodles are fine. The other ingredients are readily available in most supermarkets.

1. First of all, cut the cod into 8 equal pieces measuring about 1½ x 2 inches, then mix these with the soy sauce, fish sauce, and 2 tablespoons of water in a medium bowl. Now stir the cod around, cover it with plastic wrap, and refrigerate to marinate for about an hour, stirring it around once or twice in that time.

2. While the fish is marinating, make the soba noodle salad. As for pasta, have plenty of water boiling in a large saucepan with a little salt added. Boil the noodles, without a lid, for exactly 3 minutes, then drain them in a colander and run cold tap water on them while you lift and shake them with your hands. (They need to be cooled down quickly, otherwise the heat makes them sticky.) After that, shake off all the excess water and place the noodles in a bowl. Now whisk the soy sauce, lime juice, and sesame oil together and pour this over the noodles, mixing well, so they are coated in the dressing.

3. Now for the fish. Toward the end of the marinating time, place a bamboo or collapsible metal steamer over a pan of boiling water. (Preheating it will prevent the nori from sticking.) When you're ready to cook the fish, cut each of the nori sheets into quarters, then take one of them and lay it, shiny side down, on a clean, flat surface. Take a pastry brush, dip it into the fish marinade, and brush the nori. Then place a piece of cod in the center. Fold in 2 opposite sides, then brush the 2 remaining flaps with a little more of the marinade and wrap them over the fish, too, to form a tight parcel. (Don't worry if some of the fish is not covered.) Repeat this with the remaining fish and nori.

4. To cook them, place all the parcels, seam side down, in the steamer, put a lid on, and steam them for 5 minutes. Serve them with the noodles, garnished with the watercress, and hand the pickled ginger around separately.

Grilled Sea Bass
with Lentil and Tomato Salad
Serves 4

For the lentil salad

½ cup Puy lentils (no need to soak), rinsed

Salt, as needed

2 medium tomatoes

1 small red onion

1 medium red chili, halved and deseeded

2 tablespoons fresh cilantro leaves

Juice of 1 lime

Freshly ground black pepper to taste

For the fish

4 sea bass fillets (7–8 oz each)

2 teaspoons olive oil

Salt, preferably sea salt, and freshly ground black pepper, to taste

1 lime, cut into wedges, for serving

This is an very fast dish for four people that is full of color and flavor. Puy lentils, the tiny green kind, are particularly nice here because they tend to hold their shape, but any green lentil will do. Since lentils need no presoaking and cook in roughly half an hour, this is a dish you can throw together when you get home from work.

1. Begin by making the lentil salad. Place the lentils in a small saucepan with 1 cup water and a large pinch of salt. Bring them to a simmer, then gently simmer, without a lid, for about 30 minutes, or until they are tender but still have some bite and retain their shape, by which time most of the water will have been absorbed.

2. While the lentils are cooking, skin the tomatoes. Do this by placing them in a heatproof bowl and pouring boiling water on them. After exactly a minute, remove them from the water and slip off the skin (protecting your hands with a cloth if the tomatoes are hot), then halve each and squeeze out the seeds. Now chop them into small pieces. After that, chop the onion and chili very small, as well as the cilantro, and keep all this aside, covered in plastic wrap, until needed.

3. When the lentils are cooked, empty them into a bowl, and while they are still warm toss them in the lime juice. Now taste to check the seasoning and add salt and pepper if needed. Add the onion, chili, tomato, and cilantro, mix well, and leave aside in a cool place.

4. To cook the fish, you need to preheat the broiler to its highest setting for at least 10 minutes. Next, line a broiler pan with aluminum foil, brush the fish fillets on both sides with the oil, and place them on the tray flesh side up. Season with salt and freshly ground black pepper, then grill for 5 to 6 minutes, turning halfway through, or until just cooked through. Serve immediately with the salsa and some lime wedges for squeezing over the fish.

Salmon Trout

Salmon Steaks with Creamy Avocado Sauce
Serves 6

For the salmon

6 salmon steaks (6 oz each)

6 small sprigs of fresh tarragon or parsley

6 small bay leaves

1 small lemon, thinly sliced

Salt and freshly ground black pepper to taste

6 tablespoons dry white wine

For the sauce

1 ripe, good-sized avocado

1 small clove garlic, peeled

1 teaspoon sherry vinegar

Salt and freshly ground black pepper to taste

1 cup crème fraîche

1 bunch watercress or other pretty greens, for garnish

If you want to serve something really special for a summer dinner party that leaves you utterly free from any hassle, this cold salmon dish fits the bill perfectly. Although this recipe serves 6, you can in fact line up the salmon steaks in any number you like – 12 or even 24 – which makes it ideal for buffet parties and celebrations. In winter this recipe works equally well served with Parsley Sauce (page 111).

1. First of all, preheat the oven to 350°F. Take a two sheets of aluminum foil (about 12 X 36 inches) and overlap them in a large, shallow roasting pan. Wipe the pieces of salmon with paper towels and place each one on the foil. Now put a small sprig of tarragon or parsley on top of each one, along with a bay leaf and a slice of lemon (these ingredients are there simply to perfume the salmon very subtly without altering its flavor). Now season with salt and pepper, and finally spoon a tablespoon of wine over each salmon steak. Wrap up the salmon in the foil and make a pleat in the top to seal it. Place the roasting pan on the top shelf of the oven and bake for exactly 20 minutes. Remove the pan from the oven and cool the salmon inside the foil without opening it.

2. Meanwhile, prepare the sauce. Halve the avocado, remove the pit, then divide into quarters and peel off the skin, using a sharp knife if necessary. Place the flesh in a blender or food processor then, using a teaspoon, scrape the avocado skin to remove the last, greenest part and add that to the rest. Now add in the garlic clove, then measure in the sherry vinegar, add salt and pepper and blend until smooth. Next, remove the purée to a mixing bowl and simply fold in the crème fraîche until it's thoroughly blended. Taste to check the seasoning – it might need a little more vinegar. Cover the bowl with plastic wrap and refrigerate until you're ready to serve. This should be made only a few hours in advance to keep the luscious green color at its best.

3. When you're ready to serve the salmon, undo the foil and, using a sharp knife, ease off the strip of skin around the edge of each steak and discard it. Remove the herbs and lemon, transfer the fish to a serving dish, and decorate with small bunches of watercress or other leaves placed in the hollow center. Pass the sauce separately.

Chinese Steamed Trout with Ginger and Scallions

Serves 2

2 rainbow trout (8 oz each)

2 teaspoons coarse salt, preferably coarse sea salt

4 scallions

One 1 inch piece of fresh ginger, peeled and cut into thin strips

1 garlic cloves, thinly sliced

For the sauce

3 tablespoons Japanese soy sauce

3 tablespoons Chinese rice wine or dry sherry

1 teaspoon peeled, grated fresh ginger

1 teaspoon Asian dark sesame oil

½ teaspoon dark brown sugar

1 garlic clove, chopped

Trout is slightly higher in fat than salmon, but still very low compared with meat. The fat in both trout and salmon is the good kind we all need to include in our diets. If you're wondering what the pink pieces are in the photograph, they're pink scallions, sometimes available at Chinese grocers. Serve with steamed jasmine or basmati rice, if you like.

1. First of all, rinse the trout and dry them with paper towels, then sprinkle the outside of the fish with salt and set aside for 30 minutes to help firm up the flesh.

2. Meanwhile, to make the sauce, place the soy sauce, rice wine, ginger, sesame oil, brown sugar, and garlic in a small saucepan, then bring them to a simmer over medium-low heat, and simmer for 5 minutes.

3. Next, the scallions should be cut where the green and white parts meet. Cut the very green part on a sharp diagonal, making diamond shapes when opened out. The white parts should be thinly shredded lengthways.

4. When you're ready to cook the trout, wipe the salt away with some clean paper towels. Place the fish in a bamboo or collapsible metal steamer with the ginger and garlic scattered inside and over the top of the fish. Place the steamer over a pan of boiling water and steam with a lid on for exactly 15 minutes. Serve the trout with the reheated sauce poured on top and garnished with the sliced scallions.

Thai-Style Salmon Filo Pies
Serves 4

1 medium scallion, white and green parts, finely sliced

2 tablespoons chopped fresh cilantro

2 teaspoons grated fresh ginger

2 garlic cloves, crushed through a press

Grated zest and juice of 2 limes

4 tablespoons butter

4 sheets filo pastry, defrosted overnight in the refrigerator if frozen

4 center-cut fillets of salmon (4–5 oz each)

Salt and freshly ground black pepper to taste

To serve

A few sprigs of cilantro

1 lime, cut into quarters

Filo offers a light, easy wrap that dresses up just about any food. If you buy it frozen, be sure to follow package instructions for defrosting, and keep any sheets you are not working with covered with a kitchen towel, because the thin pastry dries out rapidly. Here it seals in all the delicious salmon juices, which mingle with the lime, ginger, and cilantro with marvelous results.

1. First of all, in a small bowl, mix together the scallion, cilantro, ginger, garlic, and lime zest, then stir in the lime juice. Now melt the butter in a small saucepan. Lay 1 sheet of filo out on a flat surface, with the long side facing you. Brush it all over with some of the melted butter, spread another sheet of filo on top, and brush lightly with melted butter as well. Using a pizza wheel or a very sharp knife, cut 3 inches from one end of the stacked filo, and discard this strip. Now cut the stacked filo in half to make two 7x12-inch rectangles.

2. Position one of the salmon fillets about 1 inch from the bottom of 1 filo rectangle. Season it with salt and pepper and sprinkle one quarter of the lime and herb mixture on top. Next, fold the short end of pastry up onto the salmon, then fold the long sides inward, roll the salmon over twice more only, and trim any surplus pastry (it's important not to end up with big wedges of pastry at each end). Wrap the other piece of salmon in exactly the same way. Repeat with the remaining filo, salmon, and lime and herb mixture. The salmon pies can be made to this point, loosely covered with plastic wrap, and refrigerated for about an hour before baking.

3. When you're ready to cook, preheat the oven to 375°F. Brush the pies all over with the remaining melted butter and place them on a lightly greased baking sheet. Bake the pies for 20 to 25 minutes or until the pastry is brown and crisp. Serve immediately, garnished with cilantro and lime wedges for squeezing over the fish.

Oven-Steamed Whole Salmon with Green Herb Mayonnaise

Serves 8

For the green herb mayonnaise

2 large eggs, at room temperature

2 teaspoons dry mustard

1 plump garlic clove, peeled

Salt

1¼ cups peanut or other flavorless oil

2 teaspoons white wine vinegar

1 cup fresh spinach leaves

½ cup fresh watercress leaves

½ cup fresh flat-leaf parsley leaves

2 tablespoons chopped fresh tarragon

1 tablespoon snipped fresh chives

1 tablespoon fresh lemon juice or more, as needed

Freshly ground black pepper to taste

For the fish

1 whole salmon (4 lb)

4 tablespoons butter, softened, plus extra for buttering the aluminum foil

1 small onion, thinly sliced

3 bay leaves

4 sprigs of fresh tarragon

Salt and freshly ground black pepper to taste

This salmon is cooked slowly, wrapped in foil in the oven. With skin and bones, head and tail intact, there is not only a concentration of flavors, but also a moistness that no other cooking method can produce. The best accompaniment is a sweet mayonnaise with summer herbs, which is best made the day before to allow the flavors to develop.

1. First, make the mayonnaise. Break the eggs straight into the container of a blender or food processor, sprinkle in the mustard, and add the garlic and 1 teaspoon salt. Measure the oil into a glass measuring cup, then switch the machine on. To blend everything thoroughly, pour the oil into the machine in a very steady trickle with the motor running. You must be very careful here – too much oil in too soon means the sauce will curdle. When all the oil is in, add the vinegar and blend. Then switch off and season to taste with salt and black pepper.

2. Now rinse the spinach, watercress, and parsley under cold water and put these into a medium saucepan. With the heat turned to medium, stir the leaves around until everything has just wilted, then tip them into a colander and rinse under cold water to set the color. Now squeeze out the excess moisture very carefully, thoroughly pressing and squeezing with a wooden spoon. Then transfer the cooked leaves to the mayonnaise with the chopped tarragon and chives and process until smooth and green. There will be some fine specks but that's okay. Now do a bit of tasting and season with lemon juice, salt, and pepper. Cover and refrigerate the mayonnaise until ready to serve.

3. When you are ready to cook the salmon, preheat the oven to 275°F. Start by wiping the fish with some damp paper towels, then place it in the center of a large double sheet of foil, generously buttered. Put half the butter, the onion slices, bay leaves, and tarragon sprigs into the center cavity of the fish, along with a seasoning of salt and pepper. The rest of the butter should be smeared on top. Now wrap the foil over the salmon to make a loose but tightly sealed package. Then place the foil package on a very large baking sheet, diagonally, so that it fits in the oven. If it seems a bit long, bend the tail end upwards. Bake in the center of the oven for 2½ hours.

4. After 2½ hours, remove the salmon from the oven and allow it to cool completely before serving. (It's best not to open the foil.) To serve, the skin will come off very easily if you first make a horizontal slit all along the middle of the salmon. Then just ease the fillets away from the bone. Serve with the sauce, some crisp, dressed salad leaves and cucumber, and hot buttered new potatoes or potato salad.

Note: For other weights of salmon, the cooking times are: for 2 lb, 1½ hours; for 3 lb, 2 hours; for 5 lb, 3 hours.

Poached Salmon in Champagne Sauce
Serves 6

6 center-cut salmon fillets
(6–7 oz each)

1 cup Champagne (can substitute
dry white wine)

1½ tablespoons butter, plus a little
extra for greasing

2 medium shallots, finely chopped

1½ tablespoons all-purpose flour

¾ cup heavy cream

6 teaspoons red salmon caviar,
for serving

Salt and freshly ground black
pepper to taste

Easy and elegant, this recipe can go from stovetop to table in less than 15 minutes. Accompany the salmon with steamed fingerling potatoes and baby green peas or else a green salad with plenty of cucumber and a lemony dressing.

1. First of all, smear a little butter over the base of a very large skillet that can hold the salmon in one layer, and arrange the fillets in the skillet. Now slowly pour the Champagne over the salmon (it will foam quite a lot but not to worry), then bring it to a simmer over medium heat. Because they're not going to be quite submerged, spoon the Champagne over the top of the fish before putting the lid on. Then gently poach the salmon for about 8 to 10 minutes. To check for doneness, insert the tip of a sharp knife into the thickest part of the salmon and ease the flesh back – it should be barely opaque.

2. While the salmon is poaching, melt the butter in a medium saucepan and cook the shallots in it over gentle heat for 5 to 6 minutes until softened and golden but not browned. When the salmon is cooked, carefully lift the fillets into a warmed dish with a slotted spatula, cover them with aluminum foil, and keep warm. Next, add the flour to the buttery shallot juices, stir it in, and cook for 1 to 2 minutes more. Add the salmon poaching liquid to the pan, a little at a time, then blend in the heavy cream, whisking until the sauce is smooth. Let it come to a simmer and cook for 1 to 2 minutes, then taste and season with some salt and pepper.

3. Serve the salmon on warmed plates with a little sauce spooned over and a teaspoon of caviar on top. Pass the rest of the sauce around in a warmed gravy boat.

Chilled Marinated Trout with Fresh Fennel
Serves 2

2 rainbow trout (8 oz each)

1 fennel bulb, trimmed and sliced (green tops reserved for garnish)

¾ teaspoon whole black peppercorns

¾ teaspoon coriander seeds

½ teaspoon fennel seeds

2 tablespoons extra virgin olive oil

1 small onion, finely chopped

1 garlic clove, finely chopped

1 lb ripe, red tomatoes, skinned and chopped

1 cup dry white wine

1 tablespoon fresh lemon juice

1 tablespoon white wine vinegar

½ teaspoon chopped fresh oregano

Salt and freshly ground black pepper to taste

For the garnish

2 small scallions, white and green parts, finely chopped

2 tablespoons chopped fresh parsley

Grated zest of 1 lemon

Fennel tops, chopped (from above)

Tart and aromatic, flavored with fennel and oregano, this Mediterranean treatment is a lovely way to present rainbow trout. It also makes a very appropriate main course for a warm day, and can be cooked and left to marinate, so when the time comes to serve it, you have nothing to do. Serve over Bibb lettuce as a starter or with buttered new potatoes and a tossed salad as a main course.

1. Begin by rinsing the fish in cold water and drying them with paper towels. Then warm a large skillet over a gentle heat, crush the peppercorns, coriander, and fennel seeds in a mortar, add them to the pan, and let them dry-roast for about 1 minute to draw out the flavors. Then add the olive oil, onion, and garlic and let them cook gently for about 5 minutes or until the onion is pale gold.

2. Next, add the tomatoes, wine, lemon juice, wine vinegar, and stir, and when it begins to bubble, season with salt and pepper and add the oregano. Now add the sliced fennel to the pan, followed by the trout, basting the fish with the juices. Simmer gently for 10 minutes. After that, use a pancake turner or another thin spatula and fork to turn each fish over carefully on to its other side – don't prod it or anything like that, or the flesh will break. Then cook it for another 10 minutes on the other side. Gently transfer the trout to a shallow serving dish, spoon the sauce all over, and cool. Cover with plastic wrap and leave them in a cool place.

3. If you want to make this dish the day before, that's okay, provided you keep it refrigerated and remove it an hour before serving. Either way, sprinkle each trout with the garnish (made simply by combining the scallions, parsley, lemon zest, and fennel tops) before taking them to the table.

Seared Spiced Salmon Steaks with Black Bean Salsa
Serves 6

6 salmon steaks (5–6 oz each)

3 plump garlic cloves

2 teaspoons fine salt, preferably sea salt

2 tablespoons chopped fresh cilantro

1½ inch piece of fresh ginger, peeled and grated

Grated zest of 2 limes (reserve the juice for the salsa)

A good pinch of ground cinnamon

A good pinch of ground cumin

2 tablespoons regular (not extra virgin) olive oil

Freshly ground black pepper to taste

For the salsa

½ cup dried black beans, soaked overnight in 2 cups cold water (can substitute canned beans)

12 oz ripe but firm tomatoes, skinned, deseeded, and finely chopped

1 red chili, deseeded and finely chopped

2 tablespoons fresh cilantro, finely chopped

1 medium red onion, finely chopped

1 tablespoon extra virgin olive oil

Juice of 2 limes (from above)

½ teaspoon fine salt, preferably sea salt

Salmon is a meaty fish that can stand up to a variety of seasonings. The black bean salsa looks in this recipe looks very pretty alongside the salmon and provides a marvelous contrast of flavors and textures.

1. A few hours before you want to cook the salmon, wipe each of the steaks with damp paper towels and remove any visible bones with tweezers. Place the salmon on a plate. With a pestle and mortar, crush the garlic and salt together until you have a creamy purée. (Or chop the garlic on a cutting board, sprinkle with the salt, and chop and mash them together into a paste. Scrape up the paste with the knife.) Transfer to a bowl, and add the grated ginger, cilantro, lime zest, cinnamon, and cumin, 1 tablespoon of the olive oil, and a good grinding of black pepper. Mix everything together and spread a little of this wet rub on each salmon steak. Cover with plastic wrap and set aside for the flavors to develop and permeate the salmon.

2. To make the salsa, drain and rinse the beans in plenty of cold water, put them in a saucepan with enough water to cover, bring to the boil and boil rapidly for 10 minutes. Then reduce the heat and simmer the beans for 30 minutes until tender. Drain and allow them to cool completely before adding all the other ingredients. Then let the salsa stand, covered, for several hours to allow the flavors to develop.

3. When you're ready to cook the salmon, preheat the broiler to its highest setting. Brush a large rimmed baking sheet with the remaining tablespoon of regular olive oil and put it under the broiler to heat up. When the broiler is really hot, use an oven mitt to remove the baking sheet, and place the salmon pieces on it. They will sear and sizzle as they touch the hot metal. Position the tray 3 inches from the heat and broil them for 7 minutes exactly, then check for doneness. The salmon flesh should look opaque when prodded in the thickest part with the tip of a sharp knife.

4. Remove them when the time is up and use a sharp knife to ease off the skins. Transfer to warm plates and garnish with the cilantro sprigs. Serve immediately with the black bean salsa.

Salmon Coulibiac
Serves 6

6 tablespoons butter

1 lb 4 oz salmon fillet, cut from the tail end, skinned

½ cup long-grain rice, preferably basmati

Salt

1 cup fish stock or ½ cup each bottled clam juice and water

1 medium onion, finely chopped

4 oz small white mushrooms, finely sliced

1 tablespoon chopped fresh dill

1 teaspoon lemon zest

2 tablespoons fresh lemon juice

2 large eggs, hard-boiled and roughly chopped

1½ tablespoons chopped fresh parsley

Freshly ground black pepper to taste

For the pastry

One 17.5-ounce package frozen puff pastry, defrosted

All-purpose flour, for rolling out the pastry

2 tablespoons butter, melted

1 egg, lightly beaten

Coulibiac is a French haute cuisine variation on a rustic Russian fish pastry. This is a somewhat streamlined, and utterly delectable, version. Serve it with some Foaming Hollandaise sauce (page 126) and a mixed-leaf salad tossed in a lemony dressing.

1. Preheat the oven to 350°F. Melt 2 tablespoons of the butter in a medium saucepan and stir in the rice. Then, when the rice is coated with butter, add the stock and a little salt and bring it to a simmer. Stir well, cover with a lid, and cook the rice for 15 minutes exactly. Take the pan off the heat and remove the lid, allowing the rice to cool.

2. Meanwhile, take a sheet of buttered aluminum foil, lay the salmon on it, and season with salt and pepper. Wrap it up loosely, pleating the foil at the top and folding in the edges. Place it on a baking sheet and bake for 10 minutes – the salmon only needs to be half cooked. Remove from the oven and open the foil, allowing the salmon to cool.

3. While the salmon and the rice are cooling, melt the remaining 4 tablespoons of butter in a small saucepan and gently cook the onion in it for about 10 minutes until the onion softens. Add the mushrooms and half the dill, and cook for another 5 minutes. Stir in the lemon zest and juice, and some salt and pepper, and allow this mixture to cool.

4. Next, take a large bowl and combine the salmon, broken up into large flakes, the eggs, the remaining dill, and half the parsley, and season well with salt and pepper. In another bowl, combine the rice mixture with the onion, mushrooms, and the rest of the parsley, and season this with salt and pepper, too.

5. Now for the pastry. Unfold 1 sheet of puff pastry and place it on a lightly floured surface. Roll the pastry into a 14-x10-inch rectangle. Cut off a 3-inch strip from the short side (reserve the strip for garnish), to make a 14x7 rectangle. Lightly brush the baking sheet and pastry with some of the melted butter, then place the pastry on the baking sheet. Spoon half the rice mixture along the center, leaving a gap of at least 1 inch all around. Spoon the salmon mixture on top of the rice, building it as high as possible and molding it with your hands – you're aiming for a loaf shape. Then mold the rest of the rice mixture on top of the salmon and brush the border with beaten egg.

6. Roll out and cut the second puff pastry sheet in exactly the same manner as the first to make a 14-x7-inch rectangle. If you have a lattice cutter, run it over the pastry, leaving an even margin of about 1 inch all round. Or, use a ½-inch diameter fluted cookie cutter to cut out a decorative pattern in the pastry. Brush the surface of this pastry with melted butter, then very carefully lift and cover the salmon mixture with it. The idea here is not to let the lattice open too much as you lift it, because it will open naturally as it goes over the filling. Press the edges together all around with fork to seal, then trim the pastry so that you're left with a ¾-inch border. Now, using the back edge of a knife, knock up the edges of the pastry, then crimp it all along using your thumb and the back of the knife, pulling the knife toward the filling each time as you go around. The coulibiac can be made an hour or so ahead to this point, covered loosely with plastic wrap and refrigerated.

7. When you're ready to cook the coulibiac, raise the oven temperature to 425°F, and brush all over the pastry with beaten egg and any remaining butter. And, if you feel like it, you can cut out little fish shapes from the reserved puff pastry trimmings to decorate the top. Bake the coulibiac in the upper third of the oven for 20 to 25 minutes, until golden brown. Remove it from the oven and let it rest for about 10 minutes before cutting into slices.

Salmon Cakes with Dilled Cucumber Sauce
Makes 12 (serves 3–4)

For the fish cakes

10 oz baking potatoes, such as russet, peeled and quartered

Salt

2 tablespoons mayonnaise

Freshly ground black pepper

One 15-ounce can red salmon, drained and flaked

2 large eggs, hard-boiled and chopped

6 cornichons, drained and chopped

2½ tablespoons chopped parsley

2½ tablespoons bottled capers, rinsed, patted dry, and chopped

2 tablespoons fresh lemon juice

1½ teaspoons anchovy paste or 4 anchovies, mashed up

¼ teaspoon ground mace

¼ teaspoon cayenne pepper

For the dilled cucumber sauce

1 lb cucumbers

1 tablespoon chopped fresh dill, plus a few sprigs to garnish

2 tablespoons butter

⅓ cup crème fraîche or sour cream

A little fresh lemon juice

For the coating and frying

1 large egg, beaten

1 cup matzo meal or unflavored dried breadcrumbs

2 tablespoons peanut or other flavorless oil

1 tablespoon butter

These combine salmon and creamy potato in a crisp coating, with a light summery sauce.

1. First, steam the potatoes, sprinkled with ¾ teaspoon of salt, for 25 minutes or until they are absolutely tender. Then remove them from the steamer, drain off the water, return them to the pan, and cover with a clean kitchen towel to absorb some of the steam for about 5 minutes. Now mash them to a purée with the mayonnaise, using an electric hand mixer, then add some salt and pepper. In a large mixing bowl, mix the mashed potatoes with the remaining ingredients. Mix thoroughly, then season again if it needs it. After that, cover the bowl and refrigerate for about 2 hours to become firm.

2. To make the sauce: first peel the cucumber with a potato peeler, as thinly as possible, because the green part just beneath the surface of the peel is important for the color of the sauce. Then cut the cucumber in half lengthways and use a teaspoon to remove the seeds. Now cut the cucumber into ¼-inch dice. Next, heat the butter in a smallish saucepan over a very low heat, add the diced cucumber and some salt, and toss it around in the butter. Then put a lid on and, keeping the heat as low as possible, let the cucumber sweat gently for about 10 minutes, shaking the pan from time to time to make sure none of it sticks to the bottom. As soon as the cucumber pieces are tender, stir in the crème fraîche, dill, and lemon juice. Season the sauce with more salt if it needs it and some black pepper, then warm it gently without boiling. Now spoon half the sauce into a blender or food processor, process until smooth, then mix together with the rest of the sauce and set aside.

3. When you are ready to cook the fish cakes, lightly flour a work surface, place the fish mixture on it, and, using your hands, pat and shape it into a long roll, 2–2½ inches in diameter. Now cut the roll into 12 round fish cakes – pat each one into a neat, flat shape and then dip them, one by one, first into beaten egg and then into the matzo meal, making sure they get a nice even coating all around.

4. In a large skillet, heat the oil and butter over high heat and, when it is hot, add half the fish cakes. Turn the heat down to medium and cook until golden brown, about 4 minutes on each side. Transfer them to crumpled paper towels to drain. Repeat with the other half. Serve on hot plates with the warm sauce and a sprig of dill.

Baked Trout with Chive Cream Sauce
Serves 2

2 rainbow trout (6–7 oz each)

3 tablespoons butter, 2 tablespoons chilled and 1 tablespoon melted

Salt and freshly ground black pepper to taste

⅓ cup crème fraîche

1 bay leaf

2 tablespoons snipped fresh chives

This recipe is a good one for anyone who works all day and needs to prepare a meal quickly – the whole thing takes less than 30 minutes. Serve with rice and steamed asparagus or sautéed fresh spinach.

1. First, preheat the oven to 425°F. Line a small roasting pan or baking sheet with aluminum foil and brush the foil with a little of the melted butter. Then wash the trout in cold water and dry them very thoroughly with paper towels.

2. Now place the trout in the roasting pan, brush each with the melted butter, and season with salt and pepper. Bake them, in the upper third of the oven, for about 10 to 15 minutes, until the flesh feels a bit firmer than raw when pressed with a finger.

3. While that's happening, pour the crème fraîche into a saucepan, add the bay leaf, and bring it up to simmering point. Then remove and discard the bay leaf and stir in the 2 tablespoons chilled butter and chives until the butter melts. Season with salt and pepper, and pour this mixture into a warm jug. Pour a little sauce over the fish and serve the remainder on the side.

Roasted Salmon
with a Pecorino-Pesto Crust
Serves 4

2 skinless salmon fillets (5–6 oz each, and about ¾ inch thick)

Juice of ½ lemon

Salt and freshly ground black pepper to taste

1½ tablespoons finely grated Pecorino Romano cheese

2 tablespoons pesto sauce, preferably homemade, but store-bought will do, stirred well

2 tablespoons fresh breadcrumbs

This recipe has proved to be one of the most popular fish recipes ever. The combination of fresh pesto sauce, with all its bold Italian flavors, and fresh salmon is sublime, and that's not all – the whole thing takes about 15 minutes from start to finish.

1. Begin by preheating the oven to 450°F. Line a large rimmed baking sheet with aluminum foil and lightly oil the foil. Trim the fillets, if needed. Run your hand over the surface of the fish to check for stray bones, and remove them with tweezers if you find some. Now place the fish on the prepared baking sheet and give each one a good squeeze of lemon juice and a seasoning of salt and pepper.

2. Next, mix one-third of the breadcrumbs with the pesto in a small bowl to form a paste, and spread this over both fish fillets. Mix half the cheese with the remaining breadcrumbs and scatter this over the pesto, then finish off with the remaining cheese. Now place the baking sheet on the middle shelf of the oven and cook for 10 minutes, by which time the top should be golden brown and crispy and the salmon just cooked and moist.

Thai-Style Stuffed Trout Fillets
Serves 2 as a main course or 4 as a starter

For the stuffing

1 tablespoon peanut or other flavorless oil

2 scallions, finely chopped, (including the green parts)

2 garlic cloves, crushed through a press

2 tablespoons chopped fresh cilantro

4 teaspoons grated creamed coconut (not canned cream of coconut), available at Asian grocers (optional)

2 teaspoons freshly grated ginger

Grated zest and juice of 1 lime

Salt and freshly ground black pepper to taste

For the fish

4 skinless trout fillets (3–4 oz each)

8 large lettuce leaves from a round lettuce, such as Bibb

To serve

1 lime, quartered

A few sprigs of fresh cilantro, for garnish

Because they are wrapped in lettuce leaves and steamed just long enough to cook through perfectly, these savory bundles of trout turn out moist and flavorful. If you want to prepare the recipe a couple of hours in advance, stuff the fish and refrigerate, tightly covered with plastic wrap or aluminum foil. Wrap in the lettuce leaves just before steaming. For a main course, serve with jasmine rice mixed with grated coconut.

1. To make the Thai stuffing, heat the oil in a small skillet and gently sauté the scallions and garlic for just 30 seconds. Then remove the pan from the heat and stir in the cilantro, creamed coconut, ginger, and lime zest and juice, and season with salt and pepper. Cool the stuffing completely.

2. Now lay the fillets on a work surface, skinned side up. Season each fillet with salt and pepper, then, using a small spatula, spread an equal amount of the stuffing along the length of each fillet. Now fold each fillet by tucking the thin end to the center and the thicker end on top of that to form a neat parcel.

3. Next, place the lettuce leaves in a bowl and pour some boiling water over them. Then lift them straight out, using a slotted spoon, and pat them dry with paper towels. They will now be really flexible and you can fold them around each fillet very easily, using 2 leaves for each. Fold and wrap them around securely so as not to lose any of the filling. Place the parcels in a bamboo or collapsible metal steamer over a large saucepan of boiling water. Cover with a lid and cook for exactly 8 minutes. Serve, garnished with sprigs of cilantro and lime quarters to squeeze over.

Salmon with a Saffron Couscous Crust and Tomato and Olive Vinaigrette

Serves 4

¾ cup plus 2 tablespoons couscous

¾ cup plus 2 tablespoons dry white wine

2–3 good pinches of saffron threads

Salt, preferably sea salt, and freshly ground black pepper to taste

4 skinless salmon fillets (5 oz each)

1 large egg, beaten

For the vinaigrette

8 oz ripe tomatoes, skinned, deseeded, and chopped small

½ cup pitted black olives, chopped to the same size as the tomatoes

1 plump garlic clove

1 teaspoon wholegrain mustard

1 tablespoon white wine vinegar

1 tablespoon fresh lemon juice

½ cup olive oil

1 tablespoon chopped fresh chervil or flat-leaf parsley

Salt, preferably sea salt, and freshly ground black pepper to taste

This is unusual but works like a dream and is very simple to prepare. The couscous crust encases the salmon and keeps all the fragrant juices inside intact. Served with perhaps some fresh, shelled peas, it makes a perfect main course for summer entertaining.

1. First of all, prepare the couscous – which is quite simple. Place the couscous in a bowl, then bring the wine to a simmer. Whisk the saffron into the wine, along with some salt and pepper, and pour the wine over the couscous. Then set the couscous aside until it has absorbed all the liquid, about 5 minutes. After this, fluff it by making cutting movements across and through it with a knife. Cool the couscous.

2. Now take each salmon fillet, season with salt and pepper, and dip it first into beaten egg, then sit it on top of the couscous and, using your hands, coat it on all sides, pressing the couscous evenly all around (it works in just the same way as breadcrumbs). Now place the coated fillets on a lightly greased baking sheet and, if you wish, cover with plastic wrap and keep refrigerated for a couple of hours until they're needed.

3. To make the vinaigrette, crush the garlic with 1 teaspoon of salt, using a pestle and mortar. (Or chop the garlic on a cutting board, sprinkle with the salt, and chop and mash them together into a paste. Scrape up the paste with the knife.) Transfer to a bowl and add the mustard, vinegar, and lemon juice. Whisk in the olive oil and a good seasoning of black pepper. About 30 minutes before serving, add the tomatoes, olives, and chervil or parsley.

4. When you are ready to cook the salmon fillets, preheat the oven to 375°F. Bake the salmon steaks for 15 to 20 minutes, or a little longer if the fish is very thick. Serve each one in a pool of vinaigrette, and pass the remaining vinaigrette separately.

Salmon Teriyaki with Sesame Cucumber Salad
Serves 4

For the marinade

¼ cup Japanese soy sauce

¼ cup sake (Japanese rice wine)

¼ cup mirin (Japanese sweet rice wine)

1 tablespoon peeled and grated fresh ginger

1 teaspoon light brown sugar

2 garlic cloves, crushed through a press

For the salad

2 tablespoons sesame seeds

1 cucumber

3 tablespoons Japanese soy sauce

2 teaspoons sake

2 teaspoons mirin

2 teaspoons unseasoned rice vinegar

1 teaspoon light brown sugar

For the fish

4 skinless salmon fillets (5 oz each)

Peanut or other flavorless oil for greasing the pan

A few snipped fresh chives, for garnish

I'm using salmon here, which works best, but it can be made with other fish, such as cod or haddock fillet, too.

1. To begin with, make the marinade. All you do is whisk together the soy sauce, sake, mirin, ginger, brown sugar, and garlic. Next, place the salmon fillets in a small, shallow dish and pour the marinade over them. Now cover them with plastic wrap and refrigerate for 2 hours, turning them once, halfway through the marinating time.

2. To make the cucumber salad, begin by toasting the sesame seeds. Do this by preheating a medium, heavy-based skillet over medium heat, then add the sesame seeds, moving them around in the pan to brown evenly. As soon as they begin to splutter and pop and turn golden, they're ready. This will take 1 to 2 minutes. Then transfer them to a plate. Next, cut the cucumber in half, then into quarters, and then into eighths (all lengthways). Remove the seeds, then chop each piece on the diagonal into 3-inch long strips and place them in a bowl. After that, measure the soy sauce, sake, mirin, vinegar, and sugar into a screw-top jar, shake them together thoroughly, then pour this mixture over the cucumber wedges and leave them to marinate for about 1 hour – again, giving them one good stir at halftime.

3. When you're ready to cook the salmon, preheat the broiler to its highest setting for at least 10 minutes. Brush a large rimmed baking sheet with the oil and put it under the broiler to preheat as well. When the grill is really hot, remove the baking sheet, using a thick oven mitt. Now take the salmon steaks out of the marinade (reserving it) and shake them slightly before placing them on to the baking tray. (They should sear and sizzle as they touch the hot metal.) Then position the tray about 3 inches from the heat source and grill them for 6 minutes exactly. Meanwhile, pour the marinade into a small skillet, bring it to a boil, and cook until the mixture has reduced by about one third and is syrupy. Strain this sauce through a sieve. Serve the salmon with the sauce poured on top, garnished with the chives. Sprinkle the sesame seeds over the cucumber salad and serve with the salmon.

Oily Fish & Other Seafood

Grilled Sardines
with Summer Herb Sauce
Serves 4

2 lb fresh sardines (about 12)

1½ cups packed fresh sorrel leaves, stalks removed, washed and dried

About 2 tablespoons olive oil

Salt and freshly ground black pepper to taste

For the sauce

½ cup packed fresh sorrel leaves, stalks removed, washed and dried

4 teaspoons snipped fresh chives

1 tablespoon chopped fresh tarragon

4 teaspoons chopped fresh basil

4 teaspoons chopped fresh flat-leaf parsley or chervil

3 shallots, finely chopped

1 large garlic clove, finely chopped

3 tablespoons cider vinegar

2 teaspoons balsamic vinegar

Salt and freshly ground black pepper to taste

Sardines have a very evocative flavor and aroma that perfectly suit outdoor eating. And, with the aromatic sorrel sauce using the bounty from the herb garden, this is a perfect summer meal. The stuffed sardines and sauce can easily be prepared well ahead of time and, if the coals on the barbecue are good and hot, the fish are cooked in moments. If sorrel is unavailable, use young spinach leaves mixed with some grated zest of lemon – about 1 tablespoon – for the stuffing. If it rains, the sardines will cook quite well in a broiler or on a ridged skillet for stovetop grilling.

1. First, prepare the sardines. Use a small pair of scissors to cut open the bellies and remove the innards. Then wipe them inside and out with damp paper towels and arrange them on a plate. Next, chop the sorrel leaves fairly finely, then season with salt and pepper, and use to stuff inside the bellies of the fish. Sprinkle the oil over the fish and rub it in so that they all get a good coating. Place the sardines in a special grilling basket to hold them, if you wish.

2. Now prepare the sauce by placing the sorrel leaves, along with chives, tarragon, basil, and parsley or chervil, shallots, and garlic in a gravy boat or serving bowl and add ⅓ cup boiling water, followed by the cider and balsamic vinegars. Stir well and season with salt and pepper.

3. The sardines will need very little time to cook – just 2 minutes on each side. Serve with the sauce passed separately.

Oat-Crusted Mackerel with Beet Relish
Serves 2

For the beet relish

2 medium beets, trimmed (about 6 oz)

2 shallots, finely chopped

4 cornichons (small sour pickles), drained and finely chopped

4 teaspoons bottled capers, rinsed and drained

1½ teaspoons red wine vinegar

1½ teaspoons mayonnaise

Salt and freshly ground black pepper to taste

A little chopped fresh parsley, for serving

For the fish

2 medium mackerel (7–8 oz each), boned (see page 125)

½ cup steel-cut oatmeal (often called Irish oatmeal or oat groats), available, often in bulk, at natural food stores

¼ cup all-purpose flour seasoned with salt and pepper

1 large egg, beaten

2 tablespoons peanut or other flavorless oil

Salt and freshly ground black pepper to taste

To serve

A few sprigs of fresh flat-leaf parsley, for garnish

A few lime wedges

Like fresh sardines, fresh mackerel are appearing more frequently in fish markets and supermarket seafood departments. Fresh mackerel have lovely, juicy flesh and a milder flavor than you might imagine. The beet relish can be made with freshly roasted beets you cook at home or the vacuum-packed kind that are already cooked. Any leftover relish will keep well in the refrigerator for up to 3 days.

1. Begin by making the beet relish. Preheat the oven to 400°F. Scrub the beets under cold water but do not peel them. Wrap each beet in aluminum foil and place on a rimmed baking sheet. Bake until the beets yield slightly to a squeeze (protect your fingers with a kitchen towel). Unwrap and cool completely. Slip off the skins and chop the beets into ¼-inch dice. Transfer the beets to a bowl and mix in the shallots, cornichons, capers, vinegar, and mayonnaise, then season with salt and pepper. Sprinkle with the parsley and set aside.

2. Now wipe the boned mackerel with paper towels, then place them flesh side up on a plate and season well with salt and pepper. Dip both sides into the seasoned flour, shaking off the excess flour. Now dip the flesh side only first into the beaten egg, then the oatmeal, pressing it down firmly into their flesh. Heat the oil in a very large skillet over high heat until it's shimmering hot. Add the mackerel, oatmeal side down, and cook for 2 to 3 minutes, or until they look golden and crusty when you lift them a little with a spatula. Now flip them over, using a spatula and fork, and let them cook for another 1 to 2 minutes. Transfer them to crumpled paper towels to drain briefly. Serve with the relish and some waxy potatoes, garnished with the parsley and lime wedges.

Caper-Stuffed Herrings
Serves 4

For the stuffing

1 cup fresh white breadcrumbs, made in a blender or food processor from slightly stale firm white bread

3 tablespoons finely chopped fresh parsley

1 tablespoon bottled capers, rinsed, drained, and chopped

1 teaspoon dry mustard

Grated zest of 1 lemon

Juice of ½ lemon

2 tablespoons butter

1 medium onion, finely chopped

Salt and freshly ground black pepper to taste

For the fish

4 herrings (about 8 oz each), gutted and boned

2 tablespoons butter

Small fish are fine candidates for stuffing because you get a good proportion of the savory filling to the meat. You'll be surprised at how easy it is the bone the individual fish at home. This recipe calls for herring, which is sometimes available fresh. If you can't find it, use 8 medium-sized whiting, about 5 oz each, and bake them for about the same amount of time as the herring.

1. Preheat the oven to 425°F. Generously butter a shallow baking dish to hold the fish without crowding. To make the stuffing, first mix the breadcrumbs, parsley, capers, mustard, lemon zest, and lemon juice together in a large mixing bowl. Now heat the butter in a skillet and soften the onion in it over a low heat for 10 minutes. Add the onion, together with its buttery juices, to the breadcrumb mixture, and season everything with salt and pepper.

2. Now open each herring out flat, and spread a quarter of the stuffing down one side of each one, then fold the other side back to its original shape. Using kitchen twine, tie a short length in three places around each fish to stop the filling from falling out while the herrings are cooking.

3. Then put the fish in the baking dish and dot them with butter. Bake in the upper third of the oven for 15 minutes, until the fish are beginning to brown, basting once with the buttery juice.

Grilled Tuna Steaks with Warm Cilantro-Caper Vinaigrette
Serves 2

For the vinaigrette

2 tablespoons extra virgin olive oil

1½ tablespoons roughly chopped fresh cilantro leaves

1½ tablespoons bottled capers, rinsed, drained, and patted dry

1 tablespoon white wine vinegar

1½ teaspoons teaspoon wholegrain mustard

Grated zest and juice of 1 lime

1 shallot, finely chopped

1 garlic clove, finely chopped

Salt and freshly ground black pepper to taste

For the fish

2 tuna steaks (about 8 oz each)

1 tablespoon extra virgin olive oil

Salt and freshly ground black pepper to taste

Because domestic broilers are so variable in their efficiency, a ridged stove-top skillet or griddle is a very good investment. It's particularly good for thick tuna steaks and gives those lovely charred stripes that look so attractive. Serve with steamed corn on the cob.

1. First of all, brush a ridged skillet for stovetop grilling with a little of the olive oil, then place it over very high heat and let it preheat till very hot – about 10 minutes. Meanwhile, as the skillet is heating, make the vinaigrette. Place the oil, cilantro, capers, vinegar, mustard, grated lime zest and juice, shallot, and garlic in a small saucepan and season with salt and pepper. Whisk them together over a gentle heat – no actual cooking is needed here; all this needs is to be warm.

2. Wipe the fish steaks with paper towels, then place them on a plate, brush them with the remaining olive oil, and season both sides with salt and black pepper. When the grill pan is ready, place the tuna steaks on it and give them about 2 minutes on each side for rare tuna.

3. When the tuna steaks are ready, remove them to warm dinner plates, and pour the vinaigrette over the fish.

Greek-Style Sautéed Baby Squid with Lemon and Garlic
Serves 2

1 lb small squid, cleaned

Grated zest and juice of 1 large lemon

3 garlic cloves. finely chopped

⅓ cup full-flavored olive oil, preferably Greek

3 tablespoons chopped fresh parsley

Salt and freshly ground black pepper to taste

Lemon wedges, for serving

Small, young squid are best for this quick-cooking recipe. To retain their tenderness, it is imperative to cook them for the briefest possible time, as directed in the recipe. This dish is particularly good served with a Greek salad and some warm pita bread to dip into the luscious juices.

1. All you do with the squid is pull off the tentacles and wash them, dry them with paper towels, and reserve them. Next, cut the body section into ½-inch rings and wash them under cold running water, then pat dry with paper towels. Place them in a shallow dish, adding the reserved tentacles. Squeeze the lemon juice over the squid, toss, and leave it for 5 minutes, when it will have absorbed most of the juice. Drain the squid through a colander and shake to remove excess liquid.

2. Next, heat the oil in a large skillet, add the garlic and lemon zest, cooking very slowly as the oil heats up. When the oil is really hot, add the squid and fry it in the hot oil, keeping it on the move and stirring often so it just slightly takes on color at the edges – it will only take about 1 to 2 minutes to cook.

3. Then add the parsley, salt, and pepper and serve it straight from the pan, with lemon wedges to squeeze over.

Linguine with Sardines, Capers, and Hot Pepper
Serves 4 to 6

1 lb dried linguine

Two 3.75-ounce cans sardines in oil

1 tablespoon olive oil

1 red chili, deseeded and finely chopped

1 tablespoon bottled capers, rinsed, drained, and patted dry

1 plump garlic clove, chopped

One 14-ounce can chopped tomatoes, well drained, or 4 ripe medium tomatoes, skinned and diced

Salt and freshly ground black pepper to taste

A few fresh basil leaves, roughly torn, for garnish

Good old canned sardines are fashionable again and are an ideal pantry ingredient – great for serving on toast sprinkled with a little balsamic vinegar and lots of seasoning. This is also the perfect meal for two, made in moments and good for anyone on a tight budget. Although linguine has a lovely shape, any pasta can be used.

1. First of all, you need to cook the pasta. Always use a large cooking pot and make sure you have at least 5 quarts of water and 1 tablespoon of salt for every pound of pasta. Bring the water up to a good fierce boil before the pasta goes in and cook it for 8 to 12 minutes without a lid, until al dente.

2. Meanwhile, drain the sardines well, reserving 1 tablespoon of sardine oil, and flake the sardines into bite-sized pieces. Combine the reserved oil and olive oil in a large skillet over medium heat. Cook the garlic and chili in the oil for about 4 minutes, until softened. Add the tomatoes, sardines, and capers, and gently heat them through, stirring occasionally. Taste and season with salt and black pepper.

3. When the pasta is ready, drain it into a colander, then quickly return it to the saucepan. Add the sauce, toss it around thoroughly for 30 seconds or so, then serve in hot pasta bowls with the torn basil sprinkled over.

Baked Mackerel with Pesto-Potato Stuffing
Serves 4

4 mackerel (10 oz each), heads removed

12 oz baking potatoes, such as russet or Burbank, peeled and cut into evenly sized pieces

4 scallions, white and green parts, finely chopped

1½ slices whole-wheat bread, cubed

1 tablespoon rolled (old-fashioned) oats

2 teaspoons olive oil, plus a little for brushing

Salt and freshly ground black pepper to taste

For the pesto sauce

2 packed cups fresh basil leaves

6 tablespoons extra virgin olive oil

1 tablespoon pine nuts

1 large garlic clove, crushed through a press

Salt to taste

¼ cup freshly grated Pecorino Romano

Lemon quarters, for serving

A few sprigs of fresh flat-leaf parsley, for garnish

When impeccably fresh, mackerel is a very delicious fish, moist and flavorful, a perfect foil for the bright pesto filling. For a no-fuss meal, the mackerel can be stuffed hours in advance and just popped into the oven about half an hour before you sit down to dinner. Serve with a lemony salad.

1. First, cook the potatoes in boiling, salted water for 20 minutes. Test them with a skewer and, when they're absolutely tender, drain them well. Return them to the saucepan and cover with a clean kitchen towel to absorb some of the steam.

2. Meanwhile, make the pesto sauce. Put the basil, oil, pine nuts, and garlic together, with some salt, in the container of a blender or food processor, and blend until you have a smooth purée. Then transfer the purée to a bowl and stir in the grated Pecorino cheese. Next, add all but 1 tablespoon of the pesto to the potatoes, then use an electric hand mixer to mash them – start with a slow speed to break them up, then go on to high until you have a smooth, lump-free purée. Now fold in the scallions, taste to check the seasoning, and add more salt and pepper as needed.

3. Next, make the topping for the fish by dropping the bread into a food processor or blender with the motor switched on (clean and dry the container well first), then follow with the rolled oats until all is uniformly crumbled.

4. To prepare the fish, wipe them inside and out with paper towels and lay them on a large foil-lined baking tray, lightly oiled. Make three diagonal cuts about 1 inch in depth all along the top side of the mackerel. Spoon the pesto mash into the body cavities, pack it in neatly, then run the edges of fork along the potato to give it some texture. Now brush the surface of the fish with olive oil and scatter it with the crumbs. Add the 2 teaspoons of olive oil to the reserved pesto and drizzle it over the crumbs, using a teaspoon. Now it's ready for the oven: bake for 25 minutes in the upper third of the oven, until the mackerel flesh looks opaque when prodded with the tip of a sharp knife at one of the diagonal cuts. Garnish with the parsley sprigs and serve with the lemon quarters for squeezing over the fish.

Grilled Squid with Spicy Tomato Jam
Serves 4 as a starter

For the jam

1 lb very ripe tomatoes

1½ medium red chilies, deseeded and roughly chopped

One 1 inch piece of fresh ginger, peeled and roughly chopped

2 garlic cloves, roughly chopped

1 tablespoon Thai fish sauce

1 cup packed dark brown sugar

¼ cup red wine vinegar

1 tablespoon balsamic vinegar

For the fish

1 lb small squid, cleaned

2 teaspoons peanut or other flavorless oil

Salt and freshly ground black pepper to taste

Arugula leaves, for serving

Fans of Thai food will recognize this sweet-hot condiment that's good with many foods. Here it acts as a sauce for drizzling over grilled baby squid, served on a bed of arugula. The jam can be made up to three months in advance and stored in the refrigerator.

1. The jam can be prepared well in advance. Roughly chop the tomatoes. (You can leave on their skins.) Then put half of them into a blender, along with the chilies, ginger, garlic, and fish sauce, and blend into a fine purée. Pour the mixture into a large saucepan. Pulse the remaining tomatoes in the blender until just chopped, not puréed. Add these to the saucepan, along with the brown sugar and red wine and balsamic vinegars, and slowly bring the mixture to a boil, stirring all the time. When the mixture reaches the boil, turn the heat down to a gentle simmer. Skim off any foam from the surface and cook gently, uncovered, for 30 to 40 minutes, stirring every 5 minutes to prevent the chopped tomato settling at the bottom. You will also need to scrape down the sides of the pan during the cooking so that everything cooks evenly. The mixture should reduce to half its volume. Now pour it into a hot, sterilized jar and close the jar with the lid and ring. Invert and allow it to cool. (You will need about one third of the jam for this recipe.)

2. Preheat a ridged skillet or griddle for stovetop grilling over high heat. Meanwhile, prepare the squid. Slit it on one side and open it out to give two flaps (retaining the tentacles). Pat dry with paper towels. (It's important that you dry the squid properly, otherwise it will stew in the pan, rather than fry.) Now, using a small sharp knife, lightly score it on the inside – if you score it on the outside, it won't curl properly. Score diagonally in one direction, then do the same in the other direction, to give little diamond shapes, taking great care not to cut right through the squid.

3. When the pan is searing hot, lightly brush the squid and the tentacles on both sides with the oil, then season with salt and pepper. Only season the squid the moment it goes into the pan – if you do it in advance, the salt will draw out all the moisture. Now add the squid and tentacles in batches to the hot pan and cook for 1 to 2 minutes, turning halfway through, until lightly charred. Use tongs to transfer the first batch to a warmed plate while you cook the rest. Serve warm or cold on a bed of arugula leaves with the jam.

Fried Bluefish Fillets with a Lime Pepper Crust
Serves 2

1½ teaspoons whole mixed peppercorns (a mixture of black, white, pink, and green peppercorns, often called peppercorn medley)

2 limes

2 tablespoons all-purpose flour

2 bluefish (about 8 oz each), gutted and boned (see page 125)

2 tablespoons olive oil

Salt, preferably crushed sea salt, to taste

The lime and pepper crust makes this dish fragrant and slightly crunchy. Squeeze lots of lime juice over before you start eating – it cuts through the richness perfectly. This treatment works perfectly well with catfish fillets as well.

1. First of all, crush the peppercorns with a pestle and mortar – not too fine, so they still have some texture. If you don't have a mortar, then crush them on a work surface under a small, heavy saucepan. Then grate the zest off the limes and add half of it to the peppercorns, then add the flour. Mix them all together and spread the mixture out on a flat plate. Wipe the bluefish dry with paper towels and coat the flesh side with the flour-pepper mixture. Press well into the fish to give it a good coating – anything left on the plate can be used to dust the skin side lightly.

2. Now, in your largest skillet, heat the oil until it is very hot. Add the bluefish, flesh side down, and cook for about 2 to 3 minutes. Have a peek by lifting up the edge with a thin metal spatula – it should be golden. Then turn the fish over onto the other side and give it another 2 minutes; the flesh should be opaque when flaked with the tip of a sharp knife. Drain on crumpled paper towels or parchment paper before serving. Serve, sprinkled with salt and the remaining lime zest, and with the zested limes, cut into quarters, for squeezing over the fish.

Baked Mackerel with Herb Stuffing
Serves 2

2 tablespoons butter

3 scallions, white and green parts, chopped

1 cup fresh breadcrumbs, made from slightly stale, firm white bread

Grated zest of ½ lemon

2 teaspoons fresh lemon juice

1 tablespoon chopped fresh parsley

1 tablespoon snipped fresh chives

1 teaspoon finely chopped fresh tarragon

½ teaspoon chopped fresh thyme

Salt and freshly ground black pepper to taste

2 mackerel (about 10 oz each), gutted and boned (see page 125)

Oil for brushing the mackerel

⅔ cup plain yogurt

Mackerel has to be really fresh, so choose fish with a bright, silvery, sparkling skin that are not dull and flabby. Serve with buttered potatoes and a crisp green salad.

1. Preheat the oven to 375°F. Start by melting the butter in a small skillet and gently cook the scallions for about 2 minutes. Combine them with the breadcrumbs, lemon zest, and lemon juice and half the parsley, chives, tarragon, and thyme. Season well with salt and pepper. Pack an equal quantity of the mixture into the belly of each fish. Brush the fish with oil and season with salt and pepper. Place the mackerel in a small roasting pan, lightly oiled.

2. Bake in the upper third of the oven for 25 minutes. Stir the remaining herbs into the yogurt and season with salt and pepper. Pour over the fish and bake for 5 minutes more. Serve the fish hot with the yogurt sauce.

Salade Niçoise
Serves 4 to 6 as a light lunch

For the vinaigrette dressing

1 teaspoon salt, preferably sea salt

1 garlic clove, peeled

1¼ teaspoons dry mustard

1 tablespoon wine or balsamic vinegar

Freshly ground black pepper to taste

6 tablespoons extra virgin olive oil

2 tablespoons finely chopped fresh herbs (such as chives, tarragon, parsley, basil, chervil or mint; if using fresh oregano and thyme, use just ½ teaspoon each)

For the salad

12 oz ripe, red tomatoes

6 cups arugula, stalks removed

½ small young cucumber, cut into smallish chunks

1 lb new potatoes, cooked and sliced

4 oz fine green beans (haricots verts), cooked

4 shallots, finely chopped

Two 6-ounce cans tuna fish in olive oil, well drained

2 large eggs, hard-boiled, peeled and quartered

One 2-ounce can anchovy fillets, drained

½ cup black olives

1 tablespoon chopped fresh parsley

Nothing much has changed over the years with this dish – it is still one of the best combinations of salad ingredients ever invented. For delicious flavor, be sure to choose tuna packed in oil, preferably olive oil; the flavor and texture is far superior to water-packed. All you need to add is lots of warm, crusty French bread.

1. To make the vinaigrette dressing, start off with a pestle and mortar. First of all, crush the flakes of sea salt to a powder, then add the peeled clove of garlic and pound them together, which will immediately bring out the garlic juices and turn it into a smooth paste. (Or chop the garlic on a cutting board, sprinkle with the salt, and chop and mash them together into a paste. Scrape up the paste with the knife and transfer to a bowl.) Next, add the mustard, work that in, then add the wine or vinegar and some black pepper, and mix thoroughly until the salt dissolves. Finally, add the olive oil. Now stir the herbs into the vinaigrette – it will look rather thick but will spread itself out beautifully once you toss it into the salad. Just before you dress the salad, pour everything into a screw-top jar and shake vigorously so it's thoroughly blended.

2. For the salad, begin by preparing the tomatoes. Place them in a bowl, pour boiling water over them, then after 1 minute, drain and slip off their skins (protecting your hands with a cloth, if you need to). Now cut each tomato in half and hold each half in the palm of your hand (cut side up), then turn your hand over and squeeze gently until the seeds come out; it's best to do this over a plate to catch the seeds.

3. Now cut each tomato into quarters. Then, in a large salad bowl, arrange the tomatoes, arugula, cucumber, potatoes, beans, and chopped shallots in layers, sprinkling a little of the dressing in as you go. Next, arrange chunks of tuna and egg quarters on top, then arrange the anchovies in a crisscross pattern, followed by a scattering of olives, the chopped parsley, and a final sprinkling of dressing. Now you need to serve the salad fairly promptly and, needless to say, it needs lots of warm, crusty baguette with the very best butter to go with it.

Homemade Pickled Mackerel
Serves 6

For the marinade

2 cups white wine vinegar

1 teaspoon whole allspice berries

1 teaspoon whole coriander seeds

½ teaspoon yellow or brown mustard seeds

1 dried red chili

A few bay leaves

1–2 teaspoons light brown sugar

For the mackerel

3 mackerel (7 oz each), gutted and boned (see page 125), cut into 6 fillets

1½ tablespoons salt

2 teaspoons dry mustard mixed with 1 teaspoon water

2 dill pickles

1 small yellow onion, thinly sliced

If you think what comes out of a jar is delectable, just wait until you taste mackerel that's been pickled in your own kitchen. It's a surprisingly easy process that only requires a few days' wait so the fish fillets can marinate long enough to absorb all the flavors. Serve with buttered whole-grain bread and a nice salad, perhaps including apples and beets, for a lovely starter or light lunch.

1. First of all make the marinade in a saucepan by combining the vinegar, allspice, coriander, mustard, chili, bay leaves, and sugar with ⅔ cup water. Bring just to the boil, then simmer very gently for 5 minutes. Remove from the heat and let stand until cooled completely.

2. Meanwhile, sprinkle the mackerel with the salt and let them drain in a colander for about 3 hours. After that, rinse off the salt and dry off any excess moisture with paper towels. Now cut each dill pickle in thirds lengthways. Spread the filleted side of each fish thinly with the prepared dry mustard and place a piece of dill pickle and some slices of onion horizontally at what was the head end of each fillet. Then roll up the fillets from the head to the tail end – the skin being on the outside – and secure each roll with a wooden toothpick. Pack them into a ceramic or glass oval casserole or dish and sprinkle the remaining onion on top. Pour over the marinade, cover the dish, and put it in the coldest (usually the lowest) part of the refrigerator. The mackerel will not be ready for serving for at least 48 hours and, in fact, they will keep well for at least a week.

Smoked Fish

Smoked Haddock with Crème Fraîche
Serves 2

12–14 oz skinless smoked haddock fillets, such finnan haddie, cut into 2 serving portions

Freshly ground black pepper to taste

⅔ cup whole milk

3 tablespoons crème fraîche

1 tablespoon butter, diced

4 teaspoons snipped fresh chives

Smoked fish are not very common in the United States, but you may find them a pleasingly savory discovery. Although domestic versions are available, salted and smoked haddock are often imported from Scotland and sold under the name finnan haddie. They can sometimes be found in well-stocked fish markets. Serve this quick dish with mashed potatoes and sautéed spinach.

1. First, place the fish in a large skillet and add a little black pepper but no salt. Then pour in the milk (it won't cover the fish, but that doesn't matter), bring to a simmer and simmer gently, uncovered, for 8 to 12 minutes. You will be able to see quite clearly when they are cooked, because the whole thing will become pale and opaque.

2. Now carefully remove the fish to a plate using a slotted spatula, increase the heat, and add the crème fraîche to the pan. Continue to simmer, uncovered, for 2 to 3 minutes, until the sauce reduces and thickens slightly. Whisk in the butter and return the fish to the sauce briefly. Scatter in the chives, let it bubble for about 30 seconds, and it's ready to serve.

Smoked Fish Pie with Cheese Mashed Potato Crust
Serves 6

8 oz skinless smoked haddock fillets, such as finnan haddie

2 cups whole milk

1 bay leaf

6 black peppercorns

A few stalks of fresh parsley

1 smoked trout (about 7 oz)

8 oz smoked salmon, coarsely chopped

2 large eggs, hard-boiled and chopped

4 teaspoons bottled capers, rinsed, drained, and patted dry

4 cornichons, drained and chopped

1 tablespoon fresh lemon juice

A few sprigs of fresh watercress, for garnish

Salt and freshly ground black pepper, to taste

For the sauce

4 tablespoons butter

¼ cup all-purpose flour

⅔ cup half-and-half

3 tablespoons chopped fresh parsley

For the topping

2 lb baking potatoes, such a russet or Burbank

4 tablespoons butter

2 tablespoons crème fraîche or sour cream

¼ cup finely shredded Gruyère cheese

1 tablespoon finely grated Parmesan

With a profusion of smoked fish, capers, and cornichons (French pickles), this one-dish meal goes well beyond family fare. Be sure to serve piping hot, and garnish each portion with watercress for a spot of extra color.

1. Preheat the oven to 400°F. Arrange the smoked haddock in a baking pan, pour in the milk and add the bay leaf, peppercorns, and parsley. Bake, uncovered, in the upper third of the oven for 10 minutes. Meanwhile, remove the skin and bones from the smoked trout, then chop the fillets 1-inch pieces, along with the smoked salmon. Place all the prepared fish in a mixing bowl. Next, when the haddock is cooked, strain off the liquid and reserve it, discarding the bay leaf, parsley, and peppercorns. Then, when the haddock is cool enough to handle, remove the skin, if necessary, and flake the flesh into largish pieces, adding it to the bowl to join the rest of the fish.

2. Next, make the sauce. Do this by melting the butter in the saucepan, stir in the flour, and gradually add the fish liquid bit by bit, stirring continuously. When all the liquid is in, finish the sauce by gradually adding the half-and-half, then some salt and pepper. Simmer for 3 to 4 minutes, then stir in the chopped parsley. Now add the hard-boiled eggs, capers, and cornichons to the fish, followed by the lemon juice and, finally, the sauce. Mix it all together gently and carefully so as not to break up the fish too much, then taste and check the seasoning and pour the mixture into a buttered 2½-quart shallow baking dish.

3. Now, to make the topping, peel and quarter the potatoes, put in a steamer placed over a large saucepan of boiling water, sprinkle with a teaspoon or so of salt, put a lid on, and steam until they are absolutely tender – about 25 minutes. Then remove the potatoes from the steamer, drain off the water, return them to the saucepan, and cover with a clean kitchen towel to absorb some of the steam for about 5 minutes. Now add the butter and crème fraîche and, on the lowest speed, use an electric hand mixer to break the potatoes up, then increase the speed to high and whip them up to a smooth, creamy, fluffy mass. Taste, season well, then spread the potatoes all over the fish, making a ridged pattern with a metal spatula. Finally, sprinkle over the grated Gruyère and Parmesan cheeses. Bake in the upper third of the oven for 30 to 40 minutes, or until the top is nicely tinged brown.

Smoked Fish Cakes
Serves 4

1 lb baking potatoes, such as russet or Burbank

Salt

1 lb kipper fillets or 2 smoked trout (12 oz total)

1 large egg, hard-boiled and chopped

2 tablespoons chopped fresh parsley

1 tablespoon bottled capers, rinsed, drained, patted dry, and chopped

2 teaspoons dry mustard mixed with 1 teaspoon water

2 teaspoons grated onion (use the large holes on a box grater)

1–2 tablespoons heavy cream

Cayenne pepper

A little grated nutmeg

About 2 tablespoons peanut or other flavorless oil

About 1 tablespoon butter

Sprigs of fresh watercress, for garnish

Lemon wedges, for serving

Fish cakes are so popular you can't have too many versions, so here's another one. Traditionally made with kippers, in this recipe smoked trout works wonderfully. It blends perfectly with potatoes and eggs.

1. First, peel and quarter the potatoes, then put them in a steamer placed over a large saucepan of boiling water. Sprinkle them with about 1 teaspoon of salt, put a lid on, and steam until they are absolutely tender – about 25 minutes. Then remove the potatoes from the steamer, drain off the water, return them to the saucepan, and cover with a clean kitchen towel to absorb some of the steam for about 5 minutes. Now place the potatoes in a bowl with the egg, capers, mustard, onion, and a tablespoon of the cream.

2. Now remove the skin from the kipper or trout and flake the fish, discarding any bones, and add the flesh to the potato mixture. Beat with a fork until everything is well combined, then season to taste with cayenne and nutmeg, adding the other tablespoon of cream if the mixture seems a little dry. Then press the mixture into about 12 small cakes.

3. Next, in a large skillet, heat the oil and butter over a high heat and, when it is really hot, add half the fish cakes to the pan. Turn the heat down to medium and cook for 4 minutes on each side. Then drain on crumpled paper towels and cover loosely with aluminum foil to keep warm. Repeat with the rest of the fish cakes, adding a little more oil and butter, if needed.

4. To serve, garnish with sprigs of watercress and lemon quarters (for squeezing the juice over the fish cakes) and have cayenne pepper available for those who like it.

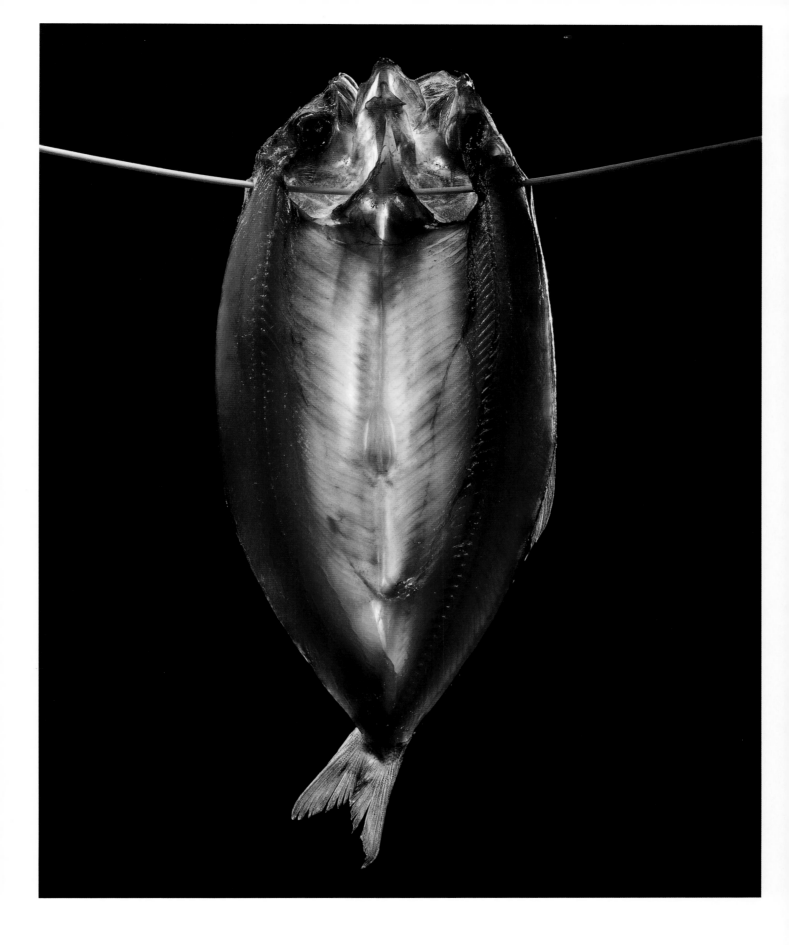

Smoked Fish Quiche
with Parmesan Crust
Serves 4 to 6

For the pastry

1 cup all-purpose flour, plus a
little extra for dusting

A pinch of salt

3 tablespoons softened vegetable
shortening

3 tablespoons softened butter

¼ cup finely grated Parmesan
cheese

For the filling

1 smoked trout (6 oz)

4 oz sliced smoked salmon,
coarsely chopped

¼ cup milk

1 bay leaf

A pinch of ground mace

2 large eggs, plus 2 egg yolks,
lightly beaten together

Freshly ground black pepper to
taste

A little ground nutmeg

¾ cup plus 2 tablespoons crème
fraîche or double cream

2 teaspoons bottled capers, rinsed,
drained, and patted dry

2 cornichons, drained and finely
chopped

Bursting with flavor, this seafood quiche makes a fine first course or light lunch. Serve with a simple green salad, dressed with a lemony vinaigrette.

1. First of all, make the pastry. Sift the flour with the pinch of salt into a large bowl, holding the sieve up high to give it a good airing. Then add the shortening and butter and, using only your fingertips, lightly and gently rub the fats into the flour, again lifting the mixture up high all the time to give it a good airing. When everything is crumbly, add the Parmesan and then sprinkle in some cold water – about 1 tablespoon. Start to mix the pastry with a knife and then finish off with your hands, adding more drops of water until you have a smooth dough that will leave the bowl clean. Then pop the pastry into a plastic bag and let it rest in the refrigerator for 30 minutes.

2. Meanwhile, preheat the oven to 375°F and place a baking sheet to preheat on the center shelf.

3. After that, roll the pastry out into a circle about 12 inches wide on a surface lightly dusted with flour and, as you roll, give it quarter turns to keep the round shape, rolling it as thinly as possible. Now transfer it, rolling it over the pin, to a 9½-inch tart pan with a removable bottom. Press it lightly and firmly all over the base and sides of the pan, easing any overlapping pastry back down to the sides, because it is important not to stretch it too much. Now trim the edges and press the pastry up about ¼ inch above the rim of the pan all around. Then prick the base all over with a fork and, after that, brush some of the beaten egg for the filling all over the base and sides. Now place the pan on the baking sheet and bake it for 20 to 25 minutes or until the pastry is crisp and golden. Check halfway through the cooking time to make sure that the pastry isn't rising up in the center. If it is, just prick it again a couple of times and press it back down again with your hands. When the pastry is baked, remove the pan from the oven and lower the temperature to 325°F.

4. For the filling, put the smoked trout in a medium saucepan, along with the milk, bay leaf, and mace. Now bring it to a simmer, cover with a lid, and poach gently for about 2 minutes. Use a slotted spoon to remove the fish from the milk. Discard the bay leaf,

but reserve the milk. Then lightly mix the eggs and egg yolks with a seasoning of black pepper and nutmeg, but no salt, since the fish will be fairly salty. Then heat the reserved milk, whisking in the crème fraîche. Then, when it has come to a simmer, pour it over the beaten eggs, whisking well.

5. Now divide the smoked trout into flakes about ½ inch in size and arrange them in the baked pastry case, along with the smoked salmon. Next, scatter the capers and cornichons all over and slowly pour in half of the cream and egg mixture, allowing the liquid to settle between each addition. Then place the baking sheet in the oven, gradually add the remainder of the filling, and cook for 30 to 35 minutes, or until the surface is golden brown and feels firm in the center.

6. When you have removed it from the oven, let it rest for 10 minutes. Ease it away from the edges using a small knife, and place the pan on a suitably sized jar, which will allow you to carefully ease the sides away. Then slide a metal spatula underneath the crust and ease the tart carefully on to a plate or board ready to serve, or simply cut it into portions straight from the tart pan base.

Smoked Fish Kedgeree with Parslied Cream Sauce
Serves 4

3 large eggs

2 cups milk

1 bay leaf

Freshly ground black pepper

1 lb skinless smoked haddock fillets, such as finnan haddie

1 smoked trout (6 oz), skinned and boned

4 oz sliced smoked salmon, coarsely chopped

1 cup basmati rice

Salt

For the parsley sauce

3 tablespoons butter

3 tablespoons all-purpose flour

1⅓ cups milk (reserved from poaching the fish)

1 cup crème fraîche or heavy cream

2 tablespoons chopped fresh parsley

This classic Anglo-Indian brunch dish uses a trio of smoked fish along with the traditional rice and eggs. Besides adding brilliant color, the sauce also makes sure the dish is moist and creamy, because the traditional version can sometimes be a bit dry.

1. Start off by boiling the eggs: the best way to achieve slightly creamy yolks is to place the eggs in cold water, bring the water to a boil, then boil them for 6 minutes. After that, cool them under cold running water. Next, place the milk in a saucepan with the bay leaf and some black pepper (don't put any salt in it because the fish is already quite salty), add the haddock, and poach it for 2 to 3 minutes after it reaches a simmer. Then add the smoked trout and smoked salmon and simmer for another minute. Now remove the bay leaf and then drain off the poaching milk – use the lid on the saucepan to enable you to strain it off through a small gap into a liquid measuring cup. Then remove the skin from the fish and divide the flesh into largish chunks. Place these in a dish, together with the peeled and halved or quartered eggs, cover with aluminum foil, and keep everything warm in a low oven. It's a good idea to pop in the serving dishes to warm as well at this stage.

2. Next, place the rice in a medium saucepan with a lid. Reserve 1⅓ cups of the poaching milk for the sauce, then add boiling water to the remaining milk to make 2 cups. Add to the rice, add ¼ teaspoon salt, and bring it to a simmer. Cover and simmer for exactly 15 minutes.

3. While that is happening, make the sauce by melting the butter in a small saucepan, then stir in the flour with a wooden spoon until you have a smooth paste. After that, add the reserved milk, a little at a time, still stirring, until you have a smooth, thickened sauce. Let it cook very gently for 2 minutes before stirring in the crème fraîche and parsley, then taste to check the seasoning.

4. Now it's an assembly job. First, place the cooked rice in a serving dish, followed by the smoked fish and eggs, and finally pour some of the sauce over – take the rest in a gravy boat to the table to allow people to help themselves.

Penne with Smoked Salmon and Mushrooms
Serves 2 as a main course or 4 as a starter

2 tablespoons butter

1 medium onion, finely chopped

1 garlic clove, crushed to a paste with 1 teaspoon salt

4 oz cremini mushrooms, thinly sliced

1 tablespoon all-purpose flour

1 teaspoon Madras-style curry powder

⅔ cup dry white wine

2 tablespoons crème fraîche or heavy cream

4 oz dried tube-shaped pasta (such as ziti, penne, or rigatoni)

8 oz smoked salmon

Salt to taste

Because this dish used bits of smoked salmon torn into strips, you can save a lot of expense by buying smoked salmon ends at delicatessens that specialize in smoked fish. They're the little pieces left over after the center fillet of the salmon is sliced, and they taste every bit as good.

1. Begin by melting the butter in a heavy skillet, then add the onion and sauté over a low heat until soft. This will take about 7 minutes. Now add the crushed garlic and mushrooms and continue to cook for a further 2 to 3 minutes. Next, mix the flour and curry powder together and stir these into the butter to soak up all the juices. Then add the wine gradually, stirring briskly after each addition and, when all the wine is added, cook for another 3 minutes before finally adding the crème fraîche. The sauce is now ready and can be made up to this stage in advance, but place a piece of plastic wrap over the surface if you're not using it immediately.

2. When you're ready to cook the pasta, place a large saucepan with plenty of lightly salted water on to boil, and cook the pasta for 10 to 12 minutes, or until it is cooked to your liking but still retains some bite. Meanwhile, tear little pieces of smoked salmon lengthways into strips, then reheat the sauce and add the salmon at the very last minute, just before serving. Now, drain the pasta, return it to the pan, then quickly stir in the sauce and smoked salmon, and serve at once in deep, heated bowls.

Marinated Smoked Salmon and Potato Salad with Coriander Seeds and Cracked Pepper

Serves 4

2 teaspoons coriander seeds

2 teaspoons whole black peppercorns

8 oz sliced smoked salmon

6 shallots or 1 medium onion, cut into thin rings

1 lemon, thinly sliced

2 bay leaves, each snipped into 3–4 pieces

A few sprigs of fresh thyme and flat-leaf parsley

Juice of 2 lemons

2½ teaspoons wholegrain mustard

1 teaspoon dark brown sugar

⅔ cup extra virgin olive oil

1 lb 8 oz small red- or white-skinned potatoes, scrubbed but skins left on

A few sprigs of fresh flat-leaf parsley, for garnish

Salt, preferably sea salt

This is a composed salad that pairs the smokiness of the fish with a pleasingly tart mustardy lemon dressing, balanced with just the right amount of sweetness. The fish can be prepared and marinated up to a week in advance.

1. To get the best fragrance from the coriander seeds and peppercorns, pop them in a small skillet and place them over a medium heat to dry-roast for 2 to 3 minutes. Move them around the skillet until they start to jump, then put them in a pestle and mortar and crush them fairly coarsely.

2. Lay the sliced salmon in a medium, nonreactive (glass or ceramic) shallow dish, sprinkling the pepper and coriander mixture all over each layer. Next, scatter the shallot or onion rings, lemon slices, bay leaves, and sprigs of thyme and parsley all over, tucking them in between the salmon here and there. In a bowl, whisk together the lemon juice, mustard, brown sugar, and oil and, when they're very thoroughly mixed, pour the mixture over the salmon. Cover with plastic wrap, and put a plate on top with some kind of weight on it to keep the salmon submerged. Place in the refrigerator and let the salmon marinate for a minimum of 24 hours or up to a week.

3. When you want to serve the salad, it's important to remove the salmon from the refrigerator at least an hour beforehand. Now steam the potatoes, generously sprinkled with salt, for 20 to 30 minutes (depending on their size). When they're cooked, remove the potatoes from the steamer, drain off the water, return them to the saucepan, and place a clean kitchen towel over them to absorb the steam for 5 minutes. Chop them roughly, divide them among the plates, spoon on some of the salmon marinade, then arrange the salmon and everything else on top. Finish off with a few sprigs of flat-leaf parsley.

Smoked Haddock with Spinach
Serves 4

For the sauce

12 tablespoons butter

3 large egg yolks

1 tablespoon fresh lemon juice

2 tablespoons chopped fresh chives

For the fish

4 pieces skinless smoked haddock fillets, such as finnan haddie (about 6 oz each)

1¼ cups milk

Freshly ground black pepper

For the spinach

2 lb spinach, picked over, trimmed, and thoroughly washed and drained

2 tablespoons butter

1 teaspoon salt

Freshly ground black pepper to taste

British food writer Simon Hopkinson was the founding chef at Bibendum, one of London's leading restaurants. This is his recipe. Serve with French bread.

1. First, you need to make the sauce: place the butter in a small saucepan and let it melt slowly over low heat. Meanwhile, blend the egg yolks, salt, and pepper in a blender or food processor. Now turn the heat up to medium-high and when the butter reaches a boil, pour it into a glass measuring cup. Start to pour the melted butter very slowly into the blender, in a thin trickle, with the motor running, until all the butter is added and the sauce is thickened. Next, with the motor still on, slowly add the lemon juice. Keep the sauce warm by placing it in a heatproof bowl over some very hot water.

2. To cook the fish, place it in a skillet, pour in the milk, add some freshly ground pepper, then bring it to a gentle simmer. Cover and poach for 6 to 7 minutes. While that is happening, cook the spinach – melt the butter in a large saucepan and pile the spinach in with the salt and some freshly ground black pepper. Put the lid on and cook it over a medium heat for 2 to 3 minutes, turning it all over halfway through. Quite a bit of water will come out, so what you need to do then is drain the spinach in a colander and press down a small plate on top to squeeze out every last bit of juice. Cover with a clean kitchen towel and keep warm.

3. When the haddock is ready, divide the spinach among 4 warm serving plates, and place the haddock pieces on top. Now just add a little of the poaching liquid (about 2 tablespoons) to the sauce and whisk it in along with the chives. Pour the sauce over the haddock and spinach. Serve immediately.

Smoked Salmon Tart
Serves 4

For the Parmesan pastry

¼ cup finely grated Parmesan cheese

1 cup plain flour

A pinch of salt

3 tablespoons softened vegetable shortening

3 tablespoons softened butter

For the filling

6 oz sliced smoked salmon, coarsely chopped

2 large eggs, plus 1 extra yolk, lightly beaten together

¾ cup plus 2 tablespoons heavy cream

Freshly grated nutmeg

A pinch of cayenne pepper

Freshly ground black pepper to taste

The secret of a great tart or quiche is a perfect pastry base – crisp, light, and flaky, without a hint of sogginess – to offset the rich, creamy filling. Here is the best of both worlds – a luscious smoked salmon tart that's simplicity itself.

1. To make the pastry, sift the flour with a pinch of salt into a large bowl, holding the sieve up high to give the flour a good airing. Then add the shortening and butter and, using only your fingertips, lightly and gently rub the fats into the flour, again lifting the mixture up high all the time to give it a good airing. Add the Parmesan and then sprinkle in some cold water – about 1 tablespoon. Start to mix the pastry with a knife and then finish off with your hands, adding more drops of water until you have a smooth dough. Place in a plastic bag and refrigerate for 30 minutes. Preheat the oven to 375°F, and place a baking sheet on the center shelf to preheat as well. Roll the pastry out into a circle about 12 inches in diameter, then roll it over the pin and transfer it to a 9½-inch tart pan with a removable bottom. Press lightly and firmly over the base and sides of the pan, pushing up the sides to come about ¼ inch above the rim of the pan all around. Now prick the base all over with a fork, then brush with some of the beaten egg for the filling. Place the pan on the preheated baking sheet and bake it for 20 to 25 minutes or until the pastry is crisp and golden. Check halfway through the baking time to make sure the pastry isn't rising in the center. If it is, just prick it a couple of times and press it back down with your hands.

2. When the pastry case is cooked, remove it from the oven and reduce the heat to 350°F. Now arrange the smoked salmon over the base of the tart. Then, in a large glass measuring cup, mix the eggs with the heavy cream and season with black pepper and a little freshly grated nutmeg, but no salt, since the smoked salmon is already quite salty. Now place the tart back on the half-pulled-out oven shelf, then pour in the egg mixture and sprinkle with the cayenne pepper. Bake it for 30 to 35 minutes until the center is just set and the surface is puffy and golden. Remove it from the oven and let it settle for about 10 minutes before serving. Remove it from the pan by placing it on an upturned jar, which will allow you to ease the sides away. Slide a metal spatula underneath the crust and ease the tart carefully on to a plate or board, ready to serve.

Finnan Haddie and Gruyère Omelette

Serves 2

2½ tablespoons crème fraîche

8 oz skinless smoked haddock fillets, cut into ½ inch chunks

5 large eggs

½ teaspoon cornstarch

1 tablespoons butter

1 teaspoon olive oil

½ cup shredded Gruyère

Salt and freshly ground black pepper to taste

This flat but fluffy open-faced omelette is a wonderful creation. If you have a black cast-iron skillet, you can serve it right out of the pan. Accompany with a tomato salad and whole-grain peasant bread.

1. To begin with, measure the crème fraîche into a medium saucepan and bring it up to a gentle simmer. Add some freshly ground black pepper, but don't add salt yet, because the haddock can be quite salty. Then pop in the prepared fish and let it poach gently, uncovered, for about 5 minutes. Meanwhile, make up the sauce: separate one of the eggs, breaking the yolk into a small bowl and reserving the white in another bowl. Add the cornstarch to the yolk and whisk well.

2. When the fish is cooked, use a slotted spoon to lift it out into a sieve placed over the saucepan, to allow the liquid to drain back. Press lightly to extract every last drop, then place the sieve containing the fish on a plate. Now bring the liquid in the saucepan back up to simmering point, then pour it on to the egg yolk, whisking all the time. Then return the whole mixture to the saucepan and gently bring it back to just below simmering or until it has lightly thickened – no more than 1 or 2 minutes. After that, remove it from the heat and stir in the fish, tasting to see if it needs any salt. Next, whisk up the egg white to the soft-peak stage and carefully fold it in.

3. Now for the omelette. At this point, preheat the broiler to its highest setting. Beat the 4 remaining eggs with some seasoning. Melt the butter and oil in an 8-inch skillet until foaming, swirling it to coat the sides and base. When it's very hot, add the

eggs, let them settle for about 2 minutes, then begin to draw the edges into the center, tilting the pan to let the liquid egg run into the gaps. When you feel the eggs are half set, turn the heat down and spoon the haddock mixture evenly over the surface of the eggs, using a spatula to spread it. Sprinkle the Gruyère on top and place the pan under the broiler, positioning it roughly 5 inches from the heat source. The omelette will take 2 to 3 minutes to become puffy, golden brown, and bubbling. Remove it and let it sit for 5 minutes before cutting into wedges and serving it on warmed plates.

Fish Extras

How to bone a whole fish

This method applies to herring, mackerel, and trout – it really is simple.

First, ask the fishmonger to scale and trim the fish. At home, all you do is cut along the belly of the fish with scissors, snipping off the head, fins, and, if you need to, the tail, then place it, flesh side down, on a flat surface.

Now, using a rolling pin, give the fish a few sharp taps to flatten it out. Next, press firmly with your thumbs or the handle of a wooden spoon **(opposite, top left)** all along the backbone of the fish, which will loosen it.

Now turn the fish skin side down and, using a sharp knife and starting at the head end, gently ease the backbone away **(top right)**; as it comes away, almost all the little bones will come away with it. Any that don't can be removed afterward, and tweezers are helpful here.

Finally, cut away the dark belly flaps, using scissors **(bottom left)**.

How to skin a fillet of fish

All you need is a flat surface and a sharp knife. First of all, angle the knife at the thinner or tail end of the fillet, or, if it's all the same thickness, just start at one end. Cut a little bit of the flesh away from the skin - enough to get the knife angled in **(opposite, bottom right)**.

Now, using your fingertips, hang on to the skin, clasping it as firmly as possible, then push the knife with your other hand, keeping the blade at an angle. Push toward the skin, not the flesh, remembering the skin is tough and the knife won't go through it. What's happening is the knife blade, as it slides between the skin and the flesh, is cutting the skin away.

If you're not experienced, don't worry if you're left with a few patches of skin - you can just gently cut these away. Practice is all you need and you'll soon be able to feel when the angle of the knife is right.

Hollandaise Sauce
Serves 4

This is supremely wonderful with any kind of grilled or poached fish.

2 large egg yolks

Salt and freshly ground black pepper to taste

1 teaspoon fresh lemon juice

1 teaspoon white wine vinegar

8 tablespoons butter

1. Begin by placing the egg yolks in a food processor or blender and season them with a pinch of salt and pepper **(opposite, top left)**. Then blend them thoroughly for about 1 minute. After that, heat the lemon juice and white wine vinegar in a small saucepan until the mixture starts to bubble and simmer **(top right)**. Switch the processor or blender on again and pour the hot liquid through the feed tube into the egg yolks in a slow, steady stream. After that, switch the processor or blender off.

2. Now, using the same saucepan, melt the butter over a gentle heat, being very careful not to let it brown. When the butter is foaming, switch the processor or blender on once more and pour in the butter in a thin, slow, steady trickle; the slower you add it, the better **(bottom left)**. If it helps you to use a pitcher and not pour from the saucepan, warm a pitcher with boiling water, discard the water, and then pour the butter into the pitcher. When all the butter has been incorporated, wipe around the sides of the processor bowl or blender with a spatula to incorporate all the sauce, then give the sauce one more quick burst and you should end up with a lovely, smooth, thick, buttery sauce **(bottom right)**.

Foaming Hollandaise

What happens here is that the egg whites from the two yolks are whisked to soft peaks and folded into the sauce as soon as it's made. The advantages are legion: first, it lightens the sauce, so there are not quite so many calories, and you get a greater volume, so it goes further. It will never curdle because the egg whites stabilize the whole thing, which means you can happily keep it warm in a bowl fitted over simmering water. That's not all: you can also reheat it in the same way and it will even freeze.

Very Quick Homemade Tartar Sauce
Serves 2 to 4

This will keep in a clean, screw-top jar in the fridge for up to a week.

1 large egg, at room temperature

1 small garlic clove, peeled

½ teaspoon dry mustard

½ teaspoon fine salt, preferably sea salt

¾ cup regular (not extra virgin) olive oil

1 tablespoon fresh flat-leaf parsley leaves

1 tablespoon bottled capers, rinsed, drained, and patted dry

4 cornichons, drained

1 teaspoon fresh lemon juice

Freshly ground black pepper to taste

Begin by breaking the egg into a processor or blender, add the garlic, mustard, and salt. Switch the motor on and, through the feed tube, add the oil in a thin, steady trickle, pouring it as slowly as you can (it takes about 2 minutes). When the oil is in and the sauce has thickened, add some pepper and all the other ingredients. Now pulse until the ingredients are chopped – as coarsely or as finely as you want. Last, taste to check the seasoning, then transfer to a serving bowl.

Cilantro and Lime Tartar Sauce

For a quick cilantro and lime tartar sauce, replace the lemon juice and parsley with lime juice and fresh cilantro. This is lovely used in Fish Fillets with Cheddar-Cilantro Crust (page 34).

Mexican Tomato Salsa
Serves 4

This is perfect served with plain grilled fish.

4 large, firm tomatoes, skinned and deseeded

1 fresh green chili, such as jalapeño, halved and deseeded

½ medium red onion, finely chopped

2 tablespoons chopped fresh cilantro

Juice of 1 lime

Salt and freshly ground black pepper to taste

First, using a sharp knife, chop the tomatoes into approximately ¼ inch dice. Next, chop the chili very finely before adding it to the tomatoes. Add the onion, cilantro, and lime juice, and season with salt and pepper. Mix thoroughly, then cover and set aside for about an hour before serving.

Mustard sauce
Serves 4-6

This is a good sauce to serve with oily fish and is particularly excellent as an accompaniment to herrings.

1¼ cup milk

1 small onion, halved

3 tablespoons butter

¼ cup plain flour

2 rounded teaspoons dry mustard powder

⅔ cup fish or vegetable stock

1 teaspoon lemon juice

salt and cayenne pepper

First of all, pour the milk into a small saucepan and add the halved onion. Then place over a low heat and let it come very slowly up to simmering point, which will take approximately 5 minutes. Then remove the saucepan from the heat and leave the milk to infuse until cooled before straining, discarding the onion.

Now place the milk, together with the butter, flour, mustard powder and stock, into the same washed pan, and bring to the boil whisking continuously. Then cook the sauce gently for 5 minutes. Taste and season with the lemon juice, salt and cayenne.

Tomato and Pesto Sauce
Serves 4

Serve with with grilled, fried, or baked fish.

1 lb skinned, chopped tomatoes

4 oz fresh pesto sauce

salt and freshly ground black pepper

All you do is place the tomatoes in a saucepan with some seasoning, simmer uncovered, and reduce until thickened for about 10 minutes. Then stir in the fresh pesto sauce, reheat gently and serve with grilled, fried, or baked fish.

Basic Fish Batter
Makes enough for four 6–7 oz pieces of fish

I have found this very simple flour and water batter is the best of all for deep-frying.

½ cup all-purpose flour

1 teapsoon baking powder

½ teaspoon salt

Just sift the flour, baking soda, and salt into a mixing bowl, then gradually add ⅔ cup water, whisking continuously until the batter is smooth and free from lumps.

Index

*Page numbers in italic refer
to photographs.*

Arugula, green herb mayonnaise 48
Avocados, salmon steaks with creamy
avocado sauce 42, *43*
Baked fish fillets with a Parmesan crust
28, 29
Baked mackerel with herb stuffing 92
Baked mackerel with pesto-potato
stuffing *84-86*, 87
Baked trout with chive cream sauce *60,* 61
Basil. *See also* Pesto
    roast cod with sun-dried tomato
    tapenade 22, *23*
Batter, basic fish 130, *131*
Beet relish *74, 75*
Bluefish, fried fillets with a lime pepper
crust *90, 91*
Capers
    caper-stuffed herring 76, *77*
    linguine with sardines, capers, and
    hot pepper *82,* 83
    warm cilantro-caper vinaigrette
    78, 79
Catfish, fried fillets with a lime pepper
crust *90,* 91
Champagne sauce *50,* 51
Cheddar cheese, seafood pie with
crisp potato topping *18,* 19
Cheese. *See* Cheddar cheese; Gruyère
cheese; Parmesan cheese; Pecorino
cheese
Chilies
    grilled squid with spicy tomato jam
    88, *89*
    linguine with sardines, capers, and
    hot pepper *82,* 83
    Mexican tomato salsa *128,* 129
    roasted monkfish with romesco sauce
    16, *17*
    Thai fish curry with mango *14,* 15
Chilled marinated trout with fresh fennel
52, *53*
Chinese steamed trout with ginger and
scallions *44,* 45
Chive cream sauce *60,* 61

Cilantro
    cilantro and lime tartar sauce 34, *35,*
    128, 129
    warm cilantro-caper vinaigrette *78,* 79
Cod
    fillets with Cheddar-cilantro crust 34, *35*
    flaky fish galette 26-27, *27*
    roasted with sun-dried tomato
    tapenade 22, *23*
    seafood pie with crisp potato topping *18,* 19
    steamed cod with nori and soba noodle
    salad *36,* 37
    teriyaki with sesame cucumber salad
    68, 69
    Thai fish cakes with sesame-lime
    dipping sauce *32,* 33
    Thai fish curry with mango *14,* 15
Condiments. See Relishes; Salsas
Conversion tables 4
Coriander, marinated smoked salmon
and potato salad with coriander seeds
and cracked pepper *114,* 115
Couscous, salmon with a saffron
couscous crust 66
Crème fraîche
    chive cream sauce *60,* 61
    creamy avocado sauce 42, *43*
    dilled cucumber sauce 58, *59*
    seafood pie with crisp potato
    topping *18,* 19
    smoked fish pie with cheese
    mashed potato crust *102,* 103
    smoked fish quiche with Parmesan
    crust 106-107, *107*
    smoked haddock with crème fraîche
    100, *101*
Cucumbers
    dilled cucumber sauce 58, *59*
    sesame cucumber salad *68,* 69
Curries
    penne with smoked salmon and
    mushrooms 112, *113*
    Thai fish curry with mango *14,* 15
Dilled cucumber sauce 58, *59*
Eggs
    finnan haddie and Gruyère omelet
    120, *121*

    salad niçoise *94,* 95
    smoked fish kedgeree with parslied
    cream sauce *108-110,* 111
    smoked fish pie with cheese mashed
    potato crust *102,* 103
Fennel, chilled marinated trout with
fresh fennel 52, *53*
Fillets of sole Véronique *10,* 11
Finnan haddie and Gruyère
omelet 120, *121*. See also Haddock,
smoked
Fish cakes
    salmon cakes with dilled cucumber
    sauce 58, *59*
    smoked fish 104
    Thai fish cakes with sesame-lime
    dipping sauce *32,* 33
Fish fillets with Cheddar-cilantro crust
34, *35*
Fish pies
    flaky fish galette 26-27, *27*
    salmon coulibiac 56-57, *57*
    seafood pie with crisp potato
    topping *18,* 19
    smoked fish pie with cheese mashed
    potato crust *102,* 103
    smoked fish quiche with Parmesan
    crust 106-107, *107*
    smoked salmon tart *118,* 119
    Thai-style salmon filo pies 46, *47*
Flaky fish galette 26-27, *27*
Flounder
    baked fillets with a Parmesan crust
    28, 29
    fillets Véronique *10,* 11
    fried fillets with herbed polenta
    crust 8, *9*
    steamed rolls with ginger, scallions,
    and sesame *24,* 25
Foaming Hollandaise sauce 56, *57,*
126, *127*
Fried bluefish fillets with a lime
pepper crust *90,* 91
Fried flounder fillets with herbed
polenta crust 8, *9*
Garlic, Greek-style sautéed baby squid
with lemon and garlic 80, *81*

Ginger
    Chinese steamed trout with ginger
    and scallions *44,* 45
    steamed fish rolls with ginger,
    scallions, and sesame *24,* 25
Grapes, fillets of sole Véronique *10,* 11
Greek-style sautéed baby squid with
lemon and garlic 80, *81*
Green beans, salad niçoise *94,* 95
Grilled sardines with summer herb
sauce 72, *73*
Grilled sea bass with lentil and tomato
salad 38, *39*
Grilled squid with spicy tomato jam 88, *89*
Grilled tuna steaks with warm cilantro-
caper vinaigrette *78,* 79
Gruyère cheese
    finnan haddie and Gruyère omelet
    120, *121*
    smoked fish pie with cheese mashed
    potato crust *102,* 103
Haddock
    flaky fish galette 26-27, *27*
    roasted with sun-dried tomato
    tapenade 22, *23*
    smoked, in finnan haddie and
    Gruyère omelet 120, *121*
    smoked, in fish kedgeree with
    parslied cream sauce *108-110,* 111
    smoked, in fish pie with cheese
    mashed potato *102,* 103
    smoked, with crème fraîche 100, *101*
    smoked, with spinach 116, *117*
    teriyaki with sesame cucumber salad
    68, 69
    Thai fish curry with mango *14,* 15
Halibut
    fillets with Cheddar-cilantro crust
    34, *35*
    seafood pie with crisp potato topping
    18, 19
    Thai fish curry with mango *14,* 15
Hazelnuts, roasted monkfish with
romesco sauce 16, *17*
Herring, caper-stuffed 76, *77*
Hollandaise sauce 126, *127*
Homemade pickled mackerel 96, *97*

Lemons, Greek-style sautéed baby squid with lemon and garlic 80, *81*
Lentil and tomato salad 38, *39*

Lime
cilantro and lime tartar sauce 34, *35*, *128*, 129
fried bluefish fillets with a lime pepper crust *90*, 91
sesame-lime dipping sauce *32*, 33
Linguine with sardines, capers, and hot pepper *82*, 83

Mackerel
baked mackerel with herb stuffing 92
baked with pesto-potato stuffing *84-86*, 87
homemade pickled mackerel 96, *97*
oat-crusted with beet relish *74*, 75

Mango, Thai fish curry with mango *14*, 15
Marinated smoked salmon and potato salad with coriander seeds and cracked pepper *114*, 115
Mexican tomato salsa *128*, 129

Monkfish
pepper-crusted with red pepper relish 30, *31*
roasted with romesco sauce 16, *17*

Mushrooms, penne with smoked salmon and mushrooms 112, *113*

Noodles and pasta
linguine with sardines, capers, and hot pepper *82*, 83
penne with smoked salmon and mushrooms 112, *113*
steamed cod with nori and soba noodle salad *36*, 37

Nori, steamed cod with nori and soba noodle salad *36*, 37
Oat-crusted mackerel with beet relish *74*, 75

Olives
roast cod with sun-dried tomato tapenade 22, *23*
salad niçoise *94*, 95
tomato and olive vinaigrette 66

Omelets, finnan haddie and Gruyère omelet 120, *121*

Oven-steamed whole salmon with green herb mayonnaise 48-49, *49*
Pan-fried skate wings with warm salsa verde 12, *13*

Parmesan cheese
baked fish fillets with a Parmesan crust *28*, 29
smoked fish pie with cheese mashed potato crust 103
smoked fish quiche with Parmesan crust 106-107, *107*
smoked salmon tart *118*, 119

Parsley
caper stuffing 76, 77
green herb mayonnaise 48
smoked fish kedgeree with parslied cream sauce *108-110*, 111

Pasta. See Noodles and pasta

Pecorino cheese
in pesto 87
roasted salmon with a Pecorino-pesto crust 62, *63*
Penne with smoked salmon and mushrooms 112, *113*

Peppercorns
fried bluefish fillets with a lime pepper crust *90*, 91
marinated smoked salmon and potato salad with coriander seeds and cracked pepper *114*, 115
pepper-crusted monkfish with red pepper relish 30, *31*
Pepper-crusted monkfish with red pepper relish 30, *31*

Pesto
pesto-potato stuffing *86*, 87
roasted salmon with a Pecorino-pesto crust 62, *63*
tomato and pesto sauce 130
Poached salmon in Champagne sauce *50*, 51

Polenta, herbed 8, *9*

Potatoes
marinated smoked salmon and potato salad with coriander seeds and cracked pepper *114*, 115

mashed, in salmon cakes with dilled cucumber sauce 58, *59*
pesto-potato stuffing *86*, 87
salad niçoise *94*, 95
seafood pie with crisp potato topping *18*, 19
smoked fish pie with cheese mashed potato crust 103
Preparation techniques *124*, 125

Relishes
beet *74*, 75
red pepper 30
spicy tomato jam 88
Roast cod with sun-dried tomato tapenade 22, *23*
Roasted salmon with a Pecorino-pesto crust 62, *63*

Saffron, salmon with a saffron couscous crust and tomato and olive vinaigrette 66
Salad niçoise *94*, 95

Salads
lentil and tomato 38, *39*
niçoise *94*, 95
potato salad with coriander seeds and cracked pepper *114*, 115
sesame cucumber 68, 69
soba noodle *36*, 37

Salmon
cakes with dilled cucumber sauce 58, *59*
cooking time by weight 49
coulibiac 56-57, *57*
marinated smoked salmon and potato salad with coriander seeds and cracked pepper *114*, 115
oven-steamed whole salmon with green herb mayonnaise 48-49, *49*
penne with smoked salmon and mushrooms 112, *113*
roasted with a Pecorino-pesto crust 62, *63*
with a saffron couscous crust and tomato and olive vinaigrette 66
seared spiced steaks with black bean salsa *54*, 55
smoked, in fish pie with cheese mashed potato crust 103

smoked fish kedgeree with parslied cream sauce *108-110*, 111
smoked fish quiche with Parmesan crust 106-107, *107*
smoked salmon tart *118*, 119
steaks with creamy avocado sauce 42, *43*
teriyaki with sesame cucumber salad *68*, 69
Thai-style salmon filo pies 46, *47*

Salsas
black bean *54*, 55
Mexican tomato *128*, 129
verde 12

Sardines
grilled with summer herb sauce 72, *73*
linguine with sardines, capers, and hot pepper *82*, 83

Sauces. See also Relishes; Salsas
Champagne *50*, 51
Chinese *44*, 45
chive cream *60*, 61
cilantro and lime tartar 34, *35*, *128*, 129
creamy avocado 42, *43*
curry *14*, 15, 112, *113*
dilled cucumber 58, *59*
green herb mayonnaise 48-49
Hollandaise 56, 57, 126, *127*
lemon and chive 116, *117*
mustard 130
parslied cream *108-110*, 111
romesco 16, *17*
sesame-lime dipping *32*, 33
summer herb 72
tomato and pesto 130
very quick homemade tartar sauce *128*, 129
white 11, 19, 26, 100, 103, 111
white wine 51

Scallions
Chinese steamed trout with ginger and scallions *44*, 45
steamed fish rolls with ginger, scallions, and sesame 24, *25*

Scallops, seafood pie with crisp potato topping *18*, 19

Sea bass, grilled with lentil and tomato salad 38, *39*
Seared spiced salmon steaks with black bean salsa *54*, 55
Seeds, how to roast 52, 115
Sesame seeds
  sesame cucumber salad *68*, 69
  sesame-lime dipping sauce *32*, 33
  steamed fish rolls with ginger, scallions, and sesame *24*, 25
Shrimp, seafood pie with crisp potato topping *18*, 19
Skate, pan-fried wings with warm salsa verde 12, *13*
Smoked fish
  cakes 104
  haddock with crème fraîche 100, *101*
  haddock with spinach 116, *117*
  kedgeree with parslied cream sauce *108-110*, 111
  pie with cheese mashed potato crust 103
  quiche with Parmesan crust 106-107, *107*
  salmon tart *118*, 119
Sole or lemon sole
  baked fillets with a Parmesan crust *28*, 29
  fillets Véronique 10, 11
  fried fillets with herbed polenta crust 8
  steamed rolls with ginger, scallions, and sesame *24*, 25
Sorrel, grilled sardines with summer herb sauce 72, *73*
Spinach
  green herb mayonnaise 48
  smoked haddock with spinach 116, *117*
Squid
  Greek-style sautéed baby squid with lemon and garlic 80, *81*
  grilled with spicy tomato jam 88, 89
Steamed cod with nori and soba noodle salad *36*, 37
Steamed fish rolls with ginger, scallions, and sesame *24*, 25

Stuffings
  caper parsley 76, *77*
  herb 92
  pesto-potato *86*, 87
  sorrel 72
  Thai *64*, 65
Tapenade, sun-dried tomato 22, *23*
Thai fish cakes with sesame-lime dipping sauce *32*, 33
Thai fish curry with mango *14*, 15
Thai-stuffed trout fillets *64*, 65
Thai-style salmon filo pies 46, *47*
Tomato and pesto sauce 130
Tomatoes
  black bean salsa *54*, 55
  chilled marinated trout with fresh fennel 52, *53*
  grilled squid with spicy tomato jam 88, *89*
  how to skin 38, 95
  lentil and tomato salad 38, *39*
  linguine with sardines, capers, and hot pepper *82*, 83
  Mexican tomato salsa *128*, 129
  pepper-crusted monkfish with red pepper relish 30, *31*
  roast cod with sun-dried tomato tapenade 22, *23*
  roasted monkfish with romesco sauce 16, *17*
  salad niçoise *94*, 95
  tomato and olive vinaigrette 66
  tomato and pesto sauce 130
Trout
  baked with chive cream sauce *60*, 61
  chilled marinated trout with fresh fennel 52, *53*
  Chinese steamed trout with ginger and scallions *44*, 45
  smoked fish kedgeree with parslied cream sauce *108-110*, 111
  smoked fish pie with cheese mashed potato crust 103
  smoked fish quiche with Parmesan crust 106-107, *107*
  Thai-stuffed trout fillets *64*, 65

Tuna
  grilled steaks with warm cilantro-caper vinaigrette *78*, 79
  salad niçoise *94*, 95
Very quick homemade tartar sauce *128*, 129
Vinaigrettes 66, *78*, 79, *94*, 95
Watercress, green herb mayonnaise 48
Whiting
  caper-stuffed 76, *77*
  fillets with Cheddar-cilantro crust 34, *35*
  flaky fish galette 26-27, *27*
Yogurt, baked mackerel with herb stuffing 92

Delia Smith is an international culinary phenomenon, whose best-selling cookbooks have sold over 17 million copies.

Delia's other books include How To Cook Books One, Two and Three, her Vegetarian Collection, the Complete Illustrated Cookery Course, One Is Fun, the Summer and Winter Collections, and Christmas. Delia is the creator of Canary Catering and now runs five successful restaurants and a series of regular food and wine workshops.

She is married to the writer and editor Michael Wynn Jones and they live in England.

Visit Delia's website at www.deliaonline.com